◢ DEDICATION ◣

With love and appreciation to all of my family for being so supportive, and especially to my sisters, Margaret, Luella (Lu), Edna, Alice, and Ethel, for without them none of this would have been possible. And to my husband Bob who has been so supportive, and patient, and to all four of my children and grandchildren, and especially to Jill who has helped in so many ways and to my niece Pat for giving me the boost to get this off the ground and all those who have helped me in other and various ways. I love you.

This is a poem written by my sister, Ethel Briggs. I asked her if we could include it and she was delighted.

✎ THE HOMESTEAD SHACK ✎

Can I feel the pain it held
The fear and desperation
Could I know the courageous hearts of
Who were strangers to our nation.

The one small room, the earthen floor
The walls so frail against the night.
How could these souls survive the cold
And rise to another morning's light.

The picture in winter white
Her blood smeared hands that twist the grasses
To feed the fire in the tiny stove.
To warm them through yet another night.

But hope and love and dignity
Lay within her breast
Just waiting to be heard
As soon as as she could rest.

But now…she struggled to survive.
No time for plans or hopes or dreams
Just the awful cold and the quiet desperation

She needed time to recollect
Why they'd come at all.
To open up a better land
Where kids grew free and strong and tall.

Elfin Cove Press

www.elfincovepress.com

An Uncertain Tomorrow

Project Manager: Bernie Ornelas
Editor: Lisa McCoy
Text Design: Amy Shayne
Cover Design: Joe Drazich

Poem by permission "The Homestead Shack" by Ethel Briggs

ISBN 0944958-27-3

Printed in Canada
1 3 5 7 9 10 8 6 4 2

An Uncertain Tomorrow

She felt the stirring in her womb
In June there'd be another babe.
"Oh, God, what will we do?"
"Where is the strength I need?"

They'd buried a child in Iowa
Tiny and frail Dorthea.
But she had born another girl
They'd named her Dora Amelia.

The Lord so good, two girls, two boys
To help them carve this land.
She felt the stab of fear and pain
How could they feed another?

But she knew they would,
They always had.
This child would be loved as the others were
And they'd give it all they could.

And as the dawn began to break
On those North Dakota plains,
She fed the flames yet one more time.
And knew she'd smile again.

≼ PROLOGUE ≽

Denmark 1876

John Peter Adamson, at fifteen years old waited for his chance to escape the harshness he'd faced ever since he was four years old and his mother died giving birth to his sister. Soon afterward his father remarried and gave John to an elderly great aunt and great uncle and his older brother Per, to an uncle. The brothers were reunited years later.

John was sent from one place to another after his great aunt died, each worse than the one before. Until he ran away and made his way south to the boarder dividing free Denmark from that southern part of Denmark which was at that time occupied by Germany. The journey was long and arduous, and he was always in fear that the farmer he'd ran away from would find him, so he walked by night, finding places to rest and hide during the day. After John finally crossed the German boarder he made his way to Abenrade. Having a knack with horses he was hired by a retired German sea Captain as stable boy.

Mary Knutson who would eventually become John's wife had been left to care for her six brothers and sisters when she was but a young girl after her parents died. During this time two of her brothers took over their father's coal route and were constant pray of the German guards at the freight yards where they loaded the coal and Mary worried that her brother Frederick would loose his temper and speak to the guards in his forbidden Danish tongue. But after she was confirmed their Tanta *aunt* Dorthea took all six to live with her and Mary took a position at the Captains as the milk-maid and cooks helper. It was here where John and Mary met.

John and his brother Per had been reunited; but then Per was given tickets to America by an uncle in Iowa, but when, due to circumstances, he and his family could not go, he gave the tickets to John. They were to go to America to work for the uncle. John and Mary had three children by this time but their youngest daughter was sickly and it was thought that perhaps the change of climate in America would make her well. When they at last were ready to go, Thea, Mary's sister was to go with them but she was forced to leave her small child behind, an act she never recovered from. It was a disastrous voyage for John since he was seasick the whole way, and once they finally reached Iowa, the uncle took one look at them, his nephew John barely able to stand, a sickly child and Mary nearly due to deliver her fourth child, and turned them away. It was only by the grace of God that a man named Andrew Peterson came to their aid. One week later John and Mary's child Dora Amelia Tora died and a month later Mary gave birth to a son, Emil. Time went on and Mary delivered another child who they called Dora Amelia, and then in 1898 John and Mary and their children and Thea and the man she had married and their children moved to North Dakota to homestead.

An Uncertain Tomorrow

Mary Torbenson

Elfin Cove Press

⟫ An Uncertain Tomorrow ⟪

John Adamson stopped to stroke a small calf and let it suckle his fingers as he walked from the barn where he slept. He felt a kinship to the animals housed alongside him in the barn…his only company. He could scarcely remember keeping company with anyone else. He'd been here, working for his keep, for what seemed forever and he knew that only his own doing would end it. He was fifteen, as near as he could figure, and his plans of escape were in the making.

It was early as he grabbed the wide-tooth wooden rake and a three-tined fork and set off toward the field where the hay lay ready and waiting to be raked into furrows and then forked into shocks. The farmer could not change his mind today and put him to some other task, because the hay could wait no longer.

When John reached the edge of the field nearest the buildings, he began working his way toward a bog thick with brush and swamp grass. It was hot, even for September, and by noon when the farmer brought him a piece of stale bread smeared with rancid lard and a jug of warm water, John's skin and clothes were wet with sweat and covered in chaff. He was skin and bone, and his dark hair straggled to a ragged shirt collar. The farmer uttered one word, *"Essen"*—"Eat"— as he shoved the food and water into his hands. The farmer never talked to him as one person to another, only growled out orders, and if John misunderstood the growled-out words he was slapped or worse. He felt only hate for the man. A supper of boiled cabbage and bread would be his only when daylight was spent and the work done, but today he didn't care because today he would be gone from this place. The year was 1876. The place was Northern Denmark.

The sun was just setting in the west when John untied the thin coat from about his waist and pulled it on. He looked back at the farm buildings and seeing no one in sight he jabbed the tines of the fork into the ground and ran toward the bog.

The ground was spongy and covered with thick wet moss as he skirted the edge of the bog, darting from bush to bush until he climbed a small rise to a neighboring field. Then, running, he finally came to a narrow wagon track leading him to a dirt road. He would use the cover of night to walk the road going south to that part of Denmark occupied by Germany. There was a pale moon lighting his way.

John kept to the edge of the road, ever ready to jump into the shallow ditch alongside it. He knew the farmer and his wife had missed him by now and he wondered if they were looking for him. He envisioned the angry man mounting his horse and racing toward him, and the thought made him shudder. He wondered what tomorrow would bring.

When John was four years old, he was separated from his older brother and baby sister after their mother died. Their father remarried and for reasons they never knew, his brother was sent to an uncle and John Peter to an elderly great-aunt and great-uncle, while the baby sister stayed with their father and stepmother. John never saw his sister again, and it would be some years before he and his brother would find one another and be reunited.

The great-aunt and great-uncle raised geese, and John was put to work herding them. His great-aunt shooed the geese through the gate and into the garden where they ate the bugs and worms. She put a piece of bread in John's pocket for lunch and left him, but as soon as the old woman was out of sight the big ganders flew at him.

John threw himself to the ground and covered his head with his hands. The ganders then pulled the bread from his pocket and ate it.

When the great-aunt died, the great-uncle sold the geese and had no more use for John Peter, so he was sent to work at another place and then another, each more demanding, as he grew older. When he was ten John was sent to a farm where they raised horses and pigs. His job was to muck out the pigsties, but one day, when he entered the sty he neglected to close a low opening to the outside pigpen where the pigs rooted in the dirt. A large boar, hearing him inside, raced in. Enraged, the animal ran at John, squealing wildly. John tried to ward the animal away with a shovel, enraging the boar even more. Finally, Laureate, the old groom from the stables, rushed in and distracted the boar with a sharp stick, giving John enough time to get over the rail.

Laureate persuaded the owner of the farm to allow him to train John Peter as a second groom and handler, wanting to teach him a trade. It was while training under the supervision of the kindly old man that John learned to love horses. Unfortunately, when Laureate died, John was put to other labors and then sent off to yet another place, but he remembered the old groom's words. "Treat it with kindness and a horse will do anything you want it to."

The mottled Danish landscape lay in folds and long, low rises, offering few trees or places to hide, so John walked by night and somehow found cover before dawn. He had to leave Denmark to be safe. If he were caught, according to Danish law, he would be sent back to the place he'd run away from. His only recourse was to go south to Germany.

Before dawn one day he found an abandoned shed some distance from a field of potatoes. Opening the sagging door, he brushed away cobwebs and peered inside. Moonlight filtered through wide cracks in the walls, revealing a small pile of debris in one corner of an otherwise empty room. He hurried back to the field and on his hands and knees dug until he unearthed several potatoes, which he stuffed in his pockets. Covering where he'd dug with dry vines, John went back to the shed to hide for the day. Lying down with one arm beneath his head he brushed the dirt from a potato on his sleeve and ate it before falling asleep. Moments later he awoke at the sound of voices coming toward him.

The voices were coming closer and he heard two men discussing the potato harvest. John peered at them through a crack between the boards of the wall and saw one man stop, turn, and look back at the field; the other came nearer the shed carrying a tin pail and a jug of water. How John yearned to put his mouth to that jug and drink his fill. A moment later, the man set down the jug and what was likely their dinner by the door of the shed and walked away. The temptation to open the door and pull the jug inside was almost more than John could bear. Instead, he moved to the back wall and easily loosened a board. He slithered through the opening and, bending low, he went down a bank to where a wide hedgerow separated two fields.

Entering the hedge, he crawled along it, bending branches out of his way, until he came to a small clear patch big enough to curl his body and lie down. The cushion of leaves beneath him was dry and brittle, crackling when he moved, but unable to resist any longer, John fell fast asleep.

When he awoke he felt stiff and cramped. Sitting up with his knees raised to his chest he dug out a potato for his supper, and with nothing better to do but wait for darkness he watched the workers in the field through the leaves. When darkness fell, John emerged from the thicket, stretched, and hurried to find the road. Never straying far from it he walked the road when darkness set firmly over the land and then, as dawn approached, he looked once more for somewhere to hide.

Small settlements became more frequent the farther south he went, which posed a particular problem. John had to skirt far around them to avoid the dogs that seemed to be on constant alert. One footstep within their hearing and first one and then another would bark or howl, the uproar waking their owners who shouted into the darkness, "Who is there? Who is there?" as John Peter ran.

The nights were turning cold, and he picked up his pace to keep warm. Having eaten the potatoes from his pockets long ago he found little else besides an occasional turnip or beet forgotten in a field.

One morning, when coming over a rise, he saw a stone cottage with a lean-to and corral on one side. There was no movement about the place, but it was still early. John moved behind an outcropping of rock and, lying down on the grass, he watched and waited until his eyelids grew heavy as sleep began to overtake him. He hadn't slept in some time and going for so long with so little food was making him weak. Just as he began to drift off, the cottage door opened and a man and woman dressed for market came out. The man led a sway-backed horse from behind the lean-to and hitched it to a cart already loaded with crates. They climbed up, sitting side by side, and started off, the cart swaying back and forth on the rough track.

John Peter waited until the cart was out of sight before going toward the homestead. Just inside the open shed were two nesting boxes. A few eggs lay in a cushion of hay in the first and a black hen sat in the other. Without hesitation he took an egg from the nest. He hadn't eaten anything since the day before when he'd found a mushy turnip in a field. Making a small hole in either end of the egg, he sucked the slippery contents as they slid down his throat.

A soft moo from behind made him turn and look into the eyes of a small black-faced cow. As he stroked her face John looked at her udder. It was limp from being milked that morning, but could there be a bit left? Still stroking her gently, he moved to her udder and, bending over, he squeezed a smooth, soft teat as he gently pulled. A stream of milk splattered his foot, and he filled his tin cup. Drinking it, he filled it again until the cow's bag was empty.

He wondered if he dare lie down in the loose hay to sleep. Not knowing how long the farmer and his wife would be gone. But seeing a place behind the manger where he wouldn't be seen, he decided to chance it. The hay smelled sweet and before he knew it, John was asleep. It was late afternoon when he awoke. He listened carefully, but could hear only the scratching of a chicken at the hard ground and the swish of the cow's tail against the flies.

John Peter stood up, covered with bits of hay and feeling better, he thought, than he had in his entire life. The cow got up and stretched when he approached and offered no objection as he squeezed the warm milk again into his cup.

John was feeling pangs of guilt about the milk and eggs he'd taken. He'd been hungry all right—maybe starving—but it hadn't been his. It seemed different, somehow, from taking a potato or a turnip or even a cabbage from a field. He wanted to do something to make it right, but what? Looking about, he noticed a few sticks of wood by the cottage door and in the yard a pile of wood to be split. An ax was wedged in the chopping block. John went to work and before long, a stack of split wood reached to the eave of the cottage. He felt better and was ready to leave, so he went back to the lean-to for his cap and forked some manure left by the cow to the manure pile outside. He put on his cap and took a step when he heard the distinct rattle of iron wheels rolling over the stony track.

There was no time! He quickly stepped behind the manger and laid out flat against it.

The cart stopped in the yard; he could hear the man and his wife chatting pleasantly about their day at market, then he heard the cottage door open and close and imagined the woman having gone inside as her husband took the harness from the horse's back. A few minutes later he heard the groan of leather as the harness was hung on a peg in the wall only a few feet from where he hid, so close he hardly dared breathe. Moments later, he heard the unmistakable sound of the horse as it drank from a trough behind the barn, slobbering contentedly. Again, it was so close he could have touched it had it not been for the wall between them.

The cottage door opened again and John thought the man had gone inside. Now was his chance, he'd run for it before they came out again, but as he moved from behind the manger the cottage door opened once more and a woman's voice called, "Come, Aud." She walked toward the lean-to, the cow following close behind. John dropped down behind the manger again before she entered and listened as she took a milk stool from the wall and sat down next to the cow. Milk rang as it hit the bottom of the pail. When she'd stripped the last of the milk she hung the stool back on the wall and started to go, then hesitating, she said, "Where did this tin cup come from? We have no such cup."

What had he done—left his cup in plain sight? John could hear hurried footsteps to the cottage. He rose quickly from behind the manger and started from the lean-to but it was too late. The door of the cottage flew open and a man's voice called, "You there, stop!"

John Peter turned to face the young couple. The man was angry and the first to speak.

"What is this? Why were you hiding in our shed and where do you come from?"

There was nothing to do but tell the truth, omitting, of course, the part about running away. In an effort to soothe the man's anger he confessed his wrong. "I am sorry, sir…ma'am, I meant no harm," he said with an imploring half-smile. "I am on my way south but when I saw your cottage I thought I'd found a place to rest and perhaps something to eat. I'm afraid I ate two of your eggs and drank some milk from your cow and took my rest behind your manger. I was leaving after splitting the wood but then I heard you coming. I am not a thief, sir."

"It appears that you are when you steal my eggs and drink my milk without permission." His wife touched his sleeve.

"Lars, look…" and she pointed toward the tall stack of wood by the cottage door. "The lad did work for his food, did he not?"

The man looked at the stack of wood and said, "That's strange—I didn't even notice it. But just the same, he took without permission."

"Look at him, Lars, he's but a boy and skinny as a rail. He's half-starved."

Lars looked first at the stack of split wood and then back at John. Taking the cap from his head he ran his fingers through his hair, stalling for time as he contemplated the matter. Then with a sheepish grin he extended a hand to slap John lightly on the shoulder. "My wife is right, you did pay for the food, and I thank you for that."

"I'll do more if you like. I know how to work."

"Yes, I'm sure you do, but you've done enough." He turned to his wife. "Will supper be ready soon?"

"*Ja*, it won't be long."

Then turning to John again Lars said, "You'll take supper with Brit and me and then bed down in the spot you like so well behind the manger."

John protested halfheartedly and without success, and soon they were seated at a small square table where a simple meal of boiled cabbage and potatoes was set before them. It was his accustomed fare, but it couldn't have tasted any better than food at a king's table.

After supper there were questions to which John had no answers without giving himself away. Then Lars unwittingly provided one. "I have a brother in Vejle but that's a long way south from here."

"I believe I might find my brother there as well. I haven't seen him in a long while. But now if you don't mind I would like to rest. Are you certain that you don't mind that I sleep in your shed?"

Brit handed him his tin cup and an old woolen scarf while Lars slapped him on the back. "Not at all. We'll talk more in the morning,"

But John had other plans when he thanked Brit for the fine supper and scarf and Lars for his hospitality; minutes later, he was walking over the rise toward the road south, the warm woolen scarf covering his ears and wound about his neck. It was the last full stomach he'd have for some time to come.

He walked for days—always at night—finding shelter where he could during the day, but food was getting harder and harder to find. There were few fields growing potatoes or cabbage or other vegetables, and even those were stripped clean because winter was closing in. Skirting small settlements John was becoming braver and less particular about what he'd eat, eating discarded potato peelings or cabbage cores standing ready to be thrown to the pigs, digging roots and drinking from stagnant ponds. Milking an unsuspecting cow one night he was kicked so hard he could barely walk.

Finding nowhere to hide one morning, he returned to the road to chance walking by day. It was cold and John was shivering as the sun came up over the horizon. His coat was thin and outgrown, the sleeves above his thin wrists and the front buttoned tight across his chest. The woolen scarf tied over his faded cap and under his chin, and with his hands stuffed in his pockets he walked on.

At fifteen, John Peter had had a miserable life. There were the ruptures above his groin as reminders, gotten from working too hard and lifting too much when he was younger and had to carry heavy sacks of grain to the barn loft by climbing a ladder fastened flat against the wall while trying to keep from falling over backward.

Ruptures were the consequence. If one popped out, he had to lie on the ground until he was able to push it back into place. The pain was unbearable until he fashioned himself a sort of support belt from a length of soft leather and wound it tightly about his girth.

The sun rose higher as he walked, and by mid-morning, with nothing in sight but flat fields, John went to the side of the road and sat down in the grass. He was tired and contemplating a risky decision. Could he gather enough grass to cover himself if he were to lie down in the shallow ditch beside the road? At that moment he froze when he saw a cloud of dust and heard the distinct sound of creaking wagon wheels. Could it be…? But no, the man was singing.

John did not move as the wagon approached, nor did the man on the wagon seem to see him. He merely pulled his mule to a stop, sat looking straight ahead for a moment and then turning to John asked, "Need a lift?"

For a moment John didn't know what to say, but when the man smiled, he answered, "Yes, if it's not a bother."

"No bother. Climb up."

Lifting the reins, the man gently slapped the mule's back as he clucked, urging the mule on.

John was grateful for the ride, yet apprehensive. Was he being foolish to accept a ride from this stranger? He could have been sent by the farmer to find him and take him to the authorities. Any misgivings he had were soon dispelled when the man began to talk, first of the weather and the crops, and then he began speaking fondly of his wife and children. Mentioning with pride his old father who lived with them, he finally asked, "Do you *leben nahe*—live near?"

"*Nei*," John said, not offering any more details.

"I am going to my brother's home to stay the night and then on to Sonderborg in the morning. You are welcome to come to my brother's home as well."

"Sonderborg is on the coast, is it not?" John Peter asked, wondering if he could reach Germany going that way.

The man replied, "Sonderborg *is* on the coast. I have business there. Where do you wish to go?"

Did he dare ask how far they were from Germany and what city was nearest to Denmark's border? He had to chance it because he had to know.

"Sir?"

"Please, my name is Hulgar."

"Hulgar...I am called John Peter."

"Hello, John Peter, and what did you want to ask?"

"Could you tell me how far it is to the German border and what city lies beyond?"

"We are about fifteen kilometers to my brother's home, and the German border is another twenty kilometers beyond that. The nearest city to the border on the German side is Abenrade, a good day's walk from the border. We Danes call it Abenraa since it was on Denmark's soil before the German occupation.

They talked for a time, but at the first lull in the conversation, John's head nodded and came to rest on his chest. Hulgar nudged him and told him to climb in the back to sleep in the hay.

Some hours later, Hulgar said loudly over his shoulder, "John Peter, I will soon turn toward my brother's home. Do you wish to go?"

John sat up, momentarily bewildered; confused by the question, he asked, "Pardon me, what did you say?"

Hulgar repeated the question and John said, "I will go with you to your brother's home but then I must continue to Abenraa."

"Abenrade." Hulgar corrected. "You must not call it otherwise once you cross the German border. In the morning we can continue on together for most of the day before I leave you to go to the coast."

Somehow this was comforting to John Peter, although their acquaintance had been short. It had been many days since his journey to Germany began and now in a few days he would be crossing the border.

At the same time, in the town of Abenrade, a young girl struggled with life as it was.

Mary held little Anna in one arm as she fed coal into the firebox of the cook stove. Her brothers were late coming home and she was worried, afraid they'd been arrested and taken to the German compound. She didn't know what she would do if that happened. Sometimes she feared they were a bit too foolhardy, speaking Danish when they knew they should speak only German since the Germans forbade the Danish language to be spoken. Mary knew, too, by the talk between the two brothers when they'd come home at the end of the day that their cockiness with the German guards at the coal yard could prove dangerous.

It seemed an incredibly long while since she'd been placed in charge by circumstance, when in truth it had been but half a year since her parents died of influenza, just two weeks apart. Of the children, only Thea had gotten sick, and she recovered after weeks of fever and vomiting. Still frail, she could at least help with little Anna and the household chores.

It was Lana who Mary counted on the most. Though the two sisters were only two years apart in age, Mary, at fourteen, could knit a sock nearly as fast as her mother had, while Lana found difficulty in casting the yarn onto the needles. Sewing, however, was another matter, as Lana's accomplishments were equal to Mary's, if not better at times. It was Mary who could cook and bake the prized Danish pastries that Christian, the youngest of the boys, took to the corner and sold for two *ore*.

It had been four years since the Germans moved across their border to occupy Abenraa. Mary was ten at the time and she remembered the frightened talk, the anger, and then, the *giving in.* Somehow they'd clung to their Danish customs and language, though it was spoken only in the privacy of their homes. But at this moment, Mary couldn't help wishing they'd set the Danish language aside and spoken only German. Perhaps then she would not have to worry about her brothers.

When their father died, Frederick, the oldest brother, stepped into his father's shoes, taking the team of horses and wagon to the coal yard early each morning to load as much coal as he was allowed, having to show the vouchers from the people on his route, proving he was not taking more coal than was needed.

The German guards often accosted him with vulgar comments or harassed him because of his youth, though he worked as a man. Frederick decided that if he took his younger brother along it might make him appear older, wiser, and more responsible. Heinrich was two years younger and much smaller then Frederick. When things with the guards went as Frederick had hoped, the two brothers took the route together every day.

Mary handed Anna to her sister who sat cross-legged before the hearth stitching a waist for the exchange of eggs. Lana laid her sewing aside and took the child on her lap. Little Anna was not a well child, sickly since birth, and yet she did not get the influenza that took their parents' lives.

Mary brushed a damp curl from her forehead. Stirring the potato grout, she heard her brothers coming, and a little smile played on her lips. Roasting pork dripped fat into the fire and sizzled. The boisterous boys sniffed deeply of the aroma as they stomped the coal dust from their boots outside the door.

No sooner had they come inside than she asked, "Where have you been Frederick and you, Heinrich? Curfew was an hour ago. Were you stopped?"

"Matter of fact we were, by a German guard." Frederick said arrogantly.

"And weren't you arrested?"

Heinrich took the wind from his brother's sail when he said, "It was Kurt who made us late because it was Kurt who stopped us before curfew."

"What? And who is Kurt?"

"A young German guard. We've gotten to be friends. He doesn't like this any better than we do. He just wants to go home," said Frederick.

"Why did he stop you then?"

"Had something for us, but we had to wait until the other guards left so we could go back to the coal yard. He'd put aside a sack of coal for our fire," Heinrich said. "Than he rode with us until we were home. We were talking in the byre, but he had to go back before he was missed."

Mary fairly shouted. "He was in our byre? Are you both mad?"

"Mary, he is our friend. He will not betray us."

Hulgar turned off the road onto a narrow track, and soon they were in sight of a substantial house with pastures and a barn. Cattle grazed contentedly in their surroundings and a big black dog raced toward them, wagging his tail in recognition of his master's brother. At the house there were warm greetings all around, and they were ushered almost immediately into a large parlor where a table was being set. A number of children were running about, excited at seeing their uncle and the newcomer. Only a small girl hid behind her mother, clutching her dress and peering out from behind with a shy smile. Seeing her, Hulgar grabbed her up in his arms and twirled her around. The little girl laughed with glee at the attention of her beloved uncle.

The table was soon laden with more food than John Peter had ever seen—or at least on a table at which he was invited to sit. The children quarreled over who would sit by their uncle until their father scolded them for their behavior and each found a place and sat down. John watched as Hulgar winked first at one and then another, triggering a giggle from each one. Finally, his brother said, "Hulgar, quit teasing and let us eat."

As each bowl or platter was passed, John was encouraged to take more until his plate was full. He kept looking up as he ate, expecting at any moment to be reprimanded for eating too much. Instead he was passed more food.

They sat at the table for what seemed like hours with everyone talking and laughing, asking about Hulgar's family and of their elderly father. They tried to bring John into the conversation by asking him questions about his family and home and where he was going. Hulgar saw that he was ill at ease and excused himself to see John to the quarters where he would sleep, saying that John was very tired.

His stomach full, and wrapped in a warm quilt, John Peter was soon asleep.

The morning meal was mush and smoked sausage, and again John was encouraged to eat his fill. When it was time to go, a basket of food was set in the cart for the journey. With everyone waving good-bye, Hulgar promised to stop in on his way home, and the gray mule pulled the cart down the track to the road.

It rained all morning and Hulgar and John sat beneath an oilskin to stay dry as the mule plodded through mud. They'd pulled the basket of food up on the bench between them, and they ate when they became hungry. Hulgar's sister-in-law had provided them with bread and cheese, cold fried sausages, pickled herring, a number of pastries, and a jug of milk from their cow.

It was late in the afternoon when Hulgar told John Peter they were nearing the fork in the road where he must turn to go to the coast. "There is a village a short way beyond where I turn and because it is so late I am going on to rest for the night at a small inn there. You are welcome to do the same. I will have but a short way back to the coast road in the morning."

John's eyes were lowered as he said, "I have no money to spend for an inn." Looking up, he said, "If I could sleep in your cart with the oilskin I would be much obliged. Then I would go on my way in the morning also."

"No need, John Peter, it is but one price for the room at the inn. We could invite as many as we'd like to stay and not one cent would be added. And we have yet enough food for our supper and still more for tomorrow. What do you say?"

"You have been too kind already. I will never be able to repay you."

"John Peter, one day I may need a friend and when I do I will look you up in your fine house in Abenraa and I know you will invite me in."

John blushed. "I doubt I'll ever have a fine house but I will always be glad to give you whatever I have."

It was settled and in a little while they were warming themselves before a fire in a small room.

The morning was bathed in sunlight as the two went to the inn's byre to harness the gray mule. Hulgar stepped to the back of the cart and took a bundle wrapped in oilskin and handed it to John. "This is for you, John Peter, a gift from my brother's family and mine."

John's face became beet red as he stammered, "For me …

what…why?"

"Open it and see." Hulgar pressed the bundle into John's hands. John was motionless. Hulgar retrieved the parcel and opened it. He put a warm, brown wool coat around John's shoulders and went to tighten the cinches on the mule's harness.

John followed him. Fighting back tears, all he could say was, "Thank you, Hulgar, and thank your brother and everyone. I'll not forget you.

At the road they parted, John going one way, Hulgar the other, looking back at each other only once and waving as they drew out of sight.

John Peter was alone again. With the warm coat still about his shoulders, he stopped by a refuse bin on the outskirts of the village and discarded the old, thin coat he'd been wearing. Putting his arms through the sleeves he saw that the coat came near his knees and fit him perfectly, and he wondered whose it had been.

In the distance John saw a sign by the side of the road; as he neared it he wished he knew how to read. In Denmark, the law required everyone to be confirmed at age fourteen; this, of course, meant studying the Bible. Since the farmer for whom John worked refused to spare him the time away from his chores, he bought off the minister to falsify the records. Consequently, John Peter could neither read nor write.

There was a flurry of traffic along the road, with carts and wagons going back toward the village and others coming from it. Two boys about John's age passed him on horseback, offering him a smile as they passed. A wagon filled with crates of squawking chickens approached and the woman riding next to her husband held a squalling child on her lap. The woman smiled as if apologizing for the racket as her husband looked straight ahead.

As the day wore on John unwrapped a thick fried sausage and ate half, saving the rest for later. He was thinking about Hulgar, wondering if he would ever see him again, when he suddenly noticed a wagon loaded with heavy hog crates a short distance ahead.

There was something familiar about the sight, or perhaps it was a feeling, that brought him to a halt. The heavy-set man who was driving sat erect in the seat. As a mule and cart came up behind and threatened to pass he raised a whip, bringing it down hard on the backs of his team. John Peter cringed. There was no mistaking the farmer he'd left those many days before. John recognized the horses, a matched team of sorrels, beaten until their spirits were gone.

What should he do? There was nowhere to hide. Had the farmer passed him? No, he'd have seen him. He must have just pulled onto the roadway and stopped to repair the wagon or something.

John decided to let the farmer get out of sight before he went on, so he sat down by the edge of the road to wait, his heart thumping in his chest. He'd come all this way without being apprehended and now when he was so close he'd have to be more careful. He'd have to go back to walking by night, but where could he hide until then and where was the farmer going with his load of hogs?

Deep in thought as he watched the road ahead John Peter didn't notice a young boy and girl on horseback until they were just opposite him. Their old horse was lame, favoring one foot. John stood up and walked toward them. "What seems to be the matter?" he asked, "Is the horse lame or does he have a stone in his hoof?"

The boy answered, "He's not lame. He was sound a while ago. I don't know what's wrong with him."

John held the horse's bridle and told the children to climb down. Holding the reins, he lifted the horse's front foot and removed a stone wedged against the soft quick. Putting the foot down he said, "There you are, he'll be fine now." The children climbed back on the horse's back. "Thank you for helping us," they said in unison.

"Do you know how far it is to the German border?"

The girl looked thoughtful for a moment and said, "I cannot say how many kilometers it is, but it isn't far. You'll come to the village where we live and the border is just beyond." Then the boy, who was older, said, "Walking, I would say about two hours."

Still thinking of the farmer and his load of hogs, John asked, "Could a person sell hogs in your village?"

"Nei...that would be Abenrade. There is a stock yard where they buy and sell hogs and cattle and horses and fowl too." Touching his cap, the boy thanked John Peter again as they trotted off.

The information about the stock yards was unsettling, for now John knew his fear of being seen by the farmer would haunt him still in German-occupied Abenrade.

John could see the lighted windows of the village and in the distance small dark shapes against the horizon. Could it be Abenrade? Suddenly he knew the meaning of real fear. At the border would they ask him questions? Would he need papers to cross? Why hadn't he asked Hulgar? This was a fine time to think of these things.

The road went through the village with wide wooden walkways on either side. The few shops were closed and no one was about. Where the buildings stopped John Peter stopped as well. Across a bare expanse was a small building with a fence stretching on either side off into the distance. This was the border, but how was he to cross? The small building was dark and the gate appeared to be locked.

Making his way around the end of the building he hurried through the darkness, and when he was some distance he stopped and looked about. He hadn't aroused even a dog. Running, he made the fence and was through it before he had time to think about it. He kept up the pace until he could run no more and dropped on a mound of soft grass. Gasping for breath, he lay looking up at a starlit sky and a moon dipping to the horizon.

The farmer had looked for John Peter along the way, asking everyone he saw, but no one had seen him. He hadn't wanted to waste a trip on the boy, so he'd loaded his wagon with hogs a few weeks after John left and started for Abenrade, certain John would go there.

He hadn't planned on the trouble he'd had with his wagon along the way or a crate breaking open and losing a prize hog either, and all because of that worthless boy. When he caught him he'd beat him within an inch of his life. He'd teach him. They'd fed and clothed the urchin and had given him a place to sleep and he repaid them like this.

He reached the village at the border too late to cross, so he took a room at a house he knew. The room faced the road and had he been looking from it he'd have seen a boy pass beneath.

John knew he had to move on to take advantage of the early hour before the sun came up. If only he could reach the city and avoid the stock yard.

The landscape, a continuance of that of Denmark, allowed him to see a long way into the distance, and with the faint glow of the sun just below the horizon, he hurried on.

Small houses were already taking shape as he reached the road again. Now there were trees and manicured yards, and he kept to their cover the best he could. The houses were dark for now, but John knew that at any moment the countryside would awake and then he would encounter people with questioning eyes. If he had to speak, what would he say? He was beginning to question whether this had been a wise move, coming into German territory. He could speak the German language as well as his native Danish since two of his masters had been German. The farmer he'd left was German through and through and would not abide being spoken to in anything but German. John was fortunate to have had Laureate, the old German groom, to teach him the words.

As a lantern was lit in a nearby house John Peter heard the sound of wagon wheels on the road. Ducking behind a hedge he watched as a wagon passed and saw that it was not the farmer but a man with a load of hay. Before he had time to weigh the situation John darted from behind the hedge and jumped into the back of the wagon. He was soon burrowed beneath the hay, but where was he going?

After a time, the feel of the road beneath the wagon changed. Lifting the hay from over his head a little, John peered out to see a cobblestone street lined on either side with large buildings. A short way farther the wagon turned onto a side street and followed close behind a wagonload of honking geese in crates.

Merchants were setting up their wares along the street, some in the back of carts some in makeshift stands where the proprietors stood behind counters selling drawn ducks and geese and strings of fat sausages hanging from a pole overhead.

The wagon left the cobblestone street, still tagging along behind the load of geese. John Peter soon recognized the very place he wanted to avoid. The wagon pulled around to the side of a large cattle pen where about fifty fat steers bellowed and pawed the ground. John watched for his chance and jumped from the wagon but which way to go was the question. He was at the stock yards, and somewhere about were the hog pens and the farmer.

John stuffed his hands in the pockets of his coat and tried to look as if he belonged there by sauntering slowly along the track leading from pen to pen. Soon his nose distinguished the difference between steer manure, chicken, and hog and he knew he was going in the wrong direction. Skirting a pen of white Landrace sows, John ducked into a narrow space between two long sheds and kept going. Before taking his hands from his pockets, he put his fingers around a round, flat object and pulled it out. Staring at a gold coin, he smiled. Hulgar had put it there, knowing he would need it for food once he entered the city, and again John wondered if he would ever see his friend again to thank him. It was only the second coin he'd had and had little idea of its worth.

A track went in either direction at the end of the shed. Looking both ways he saw an open market to his left and the track leading away from the stockyards to his right. He was hungry, and the market offered something to eat for the coin. Still concerned about encountering the farmer, he was determined to wind about the outskirts of the city and enter it farther to the south.

Before stepping out from his place between the sheds John glanced back through the expanse of dim light at a row of hog pens. A man was looking in his direction, but didn't seem to see him. It was the farmer. John was almost relieved to see him and know where he was, to know he'd avoided him.

It was mid-morning when John Peter came to a number of white-fenced paddocks bordering green pastures. A stable and barns flanked the far side of the paddocks and near the stable a boy struggled for control of a fine black gelding. The horse was rearing, its feet slashing the air, while the boy pulled on the lead and shouted excitedly at the horse. John stood with white knuckles, his hands on the top rail, one foot on the bottom, ready to bolt over the fence at any moment. Unable to stand it any longer, he shouted, *"Halt Estelle!"*—Stop!—to the stable boy, but at that moment a large hand came to rest on his shoulder. Frightened, John Peter looked up to see a large man with a full, graying, black beard. The man's eyes were piercing from beneath heavy brows, and he said in a strong quiet voice, "You can do better? What is your name?

Faltering, John said, "My name is John Peter Adamson and I do think I could do better."

"Then go…let me see." Motioning to the other lad, he watched as John firmly took the horse's lead and gently calmed the gelding and then led the horse to the paddock fence where the man waited. Stroking the horse's neck, the man asked John, "Will you stay and work for me? I like how you handle horses."

It was the first time John Peter had been asked and not told to work for someone and he stammered his reply. "I…yes, I will."

"There is a comfortable room in the stable, where you can sleep, and you'll take your meals in the kitchen. The food is good and plentiful." Looking at John he added, "It seems you could stand a few good meals. Where do you come from? But seeing John's hesitation he said, "We'll talk of that later. First put the horse in the stable and come to the house. It's nearly dinnertime."

It was the last day of September, and Mary was knitting thick wool socks for Frederick and Heinrick for the cold winter. Her fingers were flying as she worked the needles, looping the yarn over with her forefinger, the little finger holding it tightly. Already she had gloves made for all the boys and mittens for Lana and Thea and herself. She'd made a pair for little Anna as well, though she would likely not be out in the cold. It was just in case…

Mary was more at ease these days since becoming acquainted with Kurt, the young German guard. Twice he had taken supper with them, each time bringing a bag of coal for their fire and a little grain for the cow. They all knew the punishment he faced if he were caught fraternizing with them. They knew, too, how lonely he was for his home and family, showing them a faded picture of his mother. Shortly after this Kurt was sent home on furlough and Mary and the others never saw him again.

Lana was kept busy sewing for first one and then another of the more affluent women in the city, and her name had been given to a German officer's wife. It was her intention that Lana come live with her to do her sewing and help in the kitchen. Lana came home crying when she learned of this. "Oh, Mary," she sobbed, "I told her *nein* but she would not listen and I was afraid because of who she is."

"Oh my, this is terrible," said Mary. "You just cannot go. You are too young to be away from home and you will be starting your confirmation classes soon. When does she expect you? Oh you poor dear…" Mary put her arms around her sister and they wept.

Thea came from the byre and hearing of the calamity said matter-of-factly, "All you have to do is tell her that you will be away at confirmation classes a good deal of the time and you'll see…she won't want you then. Not when she learns that it's one of the Danish laws that Germany agreed to."

Astonished by her words, Lana and Mary turned to look at their small sister and Mary said, "How do you know of such things?"

"I hear people talking. The same thing happened to my friend Gretta's sister. She was asked to go live in a German home to work, but she told them about her confirmation classes and then they didn't want her."

Her eyes red from crying, Lana said, "I know…I'll ask *Tanta* Dorthea to speak to the German woman and explain about confirmation."

Mary was grim. "Do you think she'll do it? *Tanta* is not very brave, you know. I think this is something we will have to do for ourselves. Tell me where the woman lives and I will go to her in the morning. I am the oldest, and you were all more or less left in my care. Yes…I will go!"

Mary waited at the entrance to the woman's home early the next morning. She hoped she was not too early, she would not want to offend her, but Mary wanted it over with. She had had a firm talk with herself about bravery and responsibility, but as she waited for the door to open she trembled all over and she thought she might be sick. A moment later the door opened and a frail woman with a pasty complexion stood before her. Mary was quick to say what she must, having rehearsed it all the way there, and the woman was gracious, saying she regretted that Lana could not work for her but perhaps she would come when confirmation classes ended.

The relief Mary felt showed in her step as she nearly skipped all the way home. Hardly dignified for a girl with her responsibilities but today she felt like just a girl.

Opening the door, she saw four pairs of questioning eyes. When they saw her smile, their faces brightened and everyone began talking at once until Mary had to shush them so she could repeat what the woman had said. She did not, however, tell them of her own trembling and fear.

Mary turned fourteen without celebration in August, and it was past time for her confirmation exercises. She had studied the Bible backward and forward, often in the early hours of dawn, but still she worried. Would she pass the exams? Reverend Pederson was a hard taskmaster but he was a good and caring man, only wanting his students to succeed.

Tanta Dorthea came the day before the confirmation ceremony, the day the members of Mary's class learned whether or not they had passed the exams. She brought a parcel wrapped in brown paper and handed it to Mary saying, "Mary, this is for you for tomorrow."

Taking the gift Mary said, "But, Tanta, I might not have passed my exams."

"I know you passed, the Reverend told me. I saw him on the way here, but I knew you had passed without being told. Now see what I have brought you and try it on."

Mary folded back the paper and held up a soft white dress with ruffles and lace, the most beautiful dress she'd ever seen. It fit perfectly when she slipped it over her head and put her arms through the sleeves. Stepping before her mother's long mirror she gazed at herself for a long moment. How elegant she felt! She wondered how she should wear her hair. Then, remembering she was not alone, she flushed and turned to her Tanta Dorthea who wore a broad smile.

"I don't know what to say. It is so beautiful and I thank you so much."

"I am so glad you like it. I wanted you to have something like your mother would have made for you. She spoke of it before she died."

Tanta Dorthea was Mary's mother's youngest sister and the only one of her family to live so near. She watched out for her sister's children from afar, not wanting them to think she did not trust their abilities. In truth, they knew she cared because when the need was greatest she was there; though she herself was widowed and childless, she had been well-provided for.

Mary resembled her Tanta in many ways, but her hair especially was like hers: thick, golden brown, and wavy, and when she was too warm it curled about her face in damp little ringlets. Mary, however, was taller and slimmer.

Tanta Dorthea spoke now in a serious tone, "Mary, what do you plan to do now that you are confirmed?"

"Do? I will do as I am now. Nothing has changed for me."

"I have been thinking about the children. Frederick is doing well on the coal delivery and Heinrick as well; however, they both will be expected to begin their studies for confirmation soon."

"Fredrick has already begun his studies, but Heinrick will not be ready for some time." Mary corrected.

"I have a big house and I would like to have the children come live with me. You as well if you like, but I thought since you are already confirmed perhaps you would want to take employment elsewhere. I have a place in mind if you care to hear about it."

Mary was shocked by her Tanta Dorthea's proposal and she stood motionless before her. Then she quickly removed the dress and laid it carefully across the bed before saying, "I appreciate your caring and your offer but I cannot shirk my responsibility. Mor and Far— Mother and Father—would be disappointed in me. I'm sorry but I can not agree to such a thing."

"Mary, please do not be angry with me," Tanta Dorthea said. "Please think about it and ask the children. It should be their choice as well. You have been doing a splendid job ever since your parents died, but, Mary, you are too young to continue with such a heavy load."

By now the children were filing in and little Anna was crying for her supper. Tanta Dorthea pulled on her gloves and gave Mary a knowing hug as she said good-bye and left.

The evening was hectic, with everything going wrong. The creamed cabbage was scorched, the potatoes were mush, and little Anna grabbed the sock she was knitting and pulled out a needle, nearly poking it in her eye, laughing as she unraveled the yarn. Christian came from the byre carrying a little dead kitten the cow had stepped on, and Lana and Thea went into hysterics. To top it off, Frederick and Heinrick were two hours late and smelling of schnapps.

"Frederick! What is the meaning of this? You are drunk!" Mary shouted angrily.

"It is not his fault," said Heinrick. "Two German soldiers were passing a *flasche* bottle between them and when they saw us they taunted Frederick and made him drink. Then they laughed and made him do it again. He was sick all the way home and I knew I must drive. I kept the team at a slow trot and drove down all the side streets I could so as to not be seen."

Frederick had sunk into a corner, his face white as he held his stomach and moaned. Mary went to him and helped him up and onto his bed, setting a large pot beside it. Turning to Lana she said, "Quick, get some water to bathe his face. And, Thea, you and Christian go to the byre and help Heinrick tend to the horses."

When they were gone Mary bathed Frederick's face as tears rolled down her cheeks.

As he walked the black gelding to an open stall in the stable, John could hardly believe his good fortune. Looking toward the large white house that sat some distance from the barns, John scowled. Was this a trick? The man had seemed to have no qualms about letting the other boy go and putting him in his place. Suddenly he wondered if he should turn around and leave. Then someone called to him from behind. "Are you going in for dinner?"

John turned and saw the boy who'd been struggling with the gelding looking anything but angry about his dismissal. "Oh, you're still here. I'm sorry that you were dismissed. I didn't mean to cause you your job."

Grinning, the other boy said, "I'm glad you did. I admit I am a bit ill at ease around horses. You see, I was kicked badly when I was small and have never quite gotten over it."

"But then why were you working as a stable boy?"

"I was not the stable boy really. I was just put in that place when Arvid, the old stable hand, passed on." The boy added, "I'm glad you came along so I can get back to my regular duties. Come on, let's get up to dinner before Dora clears everything away. She doesn't like to be kept waiting."

Entering the back of the house they were greeted cantankerously by a short, stout woman with a round, flushed face. A long, stiffly starched, white apron covering her front was stained with food, and she raised a finger and shook it at them. "Bjorn, I have told you not to be late. And who is this?" She looked at John.

"I am John Peter and I have just come to work here."

"John Peter, is it? Well, John Peter, the same goes for you." Dora turned toward a large black cook stove. It was October—not summer—and a table was set with two blue enamel plates and flatware. Dora filled a mug at each place from a gray enameled coffeepot as they sat down. Taking steaming bowls from the warming oven she set them on the table, and Bjorn began filling his plate, passing the bowls to John. John watched the quantity of Bjorn's helpings and filled his plate accordingly.

John learned during the noon meal a little of the man who'd hired him. He was referred to by both of John's new acquaintances as the "Captain," a man to be respected and obeyed but not feared, and John would soon learn this to be so.

Bjorn was left in the stable to show John his duties and to help him clean the stalls. Bjorn's expertise was not with horses, but cows, and he knew the farm's workings and the expectations of the Captain only too well.

Time passed and soon John was given more and more responsibility. The Captain observed John with the yearlings and often the colts as well. John tied a burlap bag to a horse's back, leaving it in place for several hours at a time, gradually adding weight to the bag by placing objects inside. The Captain was impressed and curious at the technique and asked, "Where did you learn to prepare the young horses—even colts—to be broken like this?"

By this time John had revealed the story of his journey from northern Denmark and felt free to tell the Captain anything he wanted to know.

"An old man by the name of Laureate taught me. I remember many things he said." John explained how he had happened to be in his charge. "He had such a way with horses and he said I was blessed with the same gift." John's face flushed. "I don't mean to brag."

Ignoring John's embarrassment, the Captain said, "He was right—you are gifted. You have a way I've seldom seen, and this way of breaking them is completely new to me." Then he said, "Carry on," and turned to go.

It was the end of winter and the streams that had been frozen were thawing rapidly and the snow was gone, leaving the paddocks near the stable and barns a muddy mess. Only the higher pastures escaped and so it was to there that John Peter led or rode the horses along a raised track.

The Captain was usually present when one of his mares was to foal. He took great pride in his horses and knew what to do if the mare needed help in the delivery. But one day his Morgan mare saw fit to foal early, and the Captain was nowhere to be found. John and Bjorn would have to see to it themselves. The mare was anxious and paced her stall until finally she lay down. A short time later, her foal was born. They watched as the foal struggled to his feet, but all was not right. The foal had a clubfoot—the foot and ankle were turned in at a grotesque angle. John was horrified as they watched the foal stumble to his mother's udder. When he was finished nursing he flopped down in the straw, and John knelt to examine the foot. Speaking to Bjorn over his shoulder, he asked him to bring two pieces of wood and some twine.

"What are you going to do, make a splint?"

"If I can," John answered.

While Bjorn was finding what he'd asked for, John was trying to right the foot by putting pressure on it. The foal thrashed about from the pain and the mare became agitated, so John led the big mare to another stall some distance away, where she paced and snorted excitedly. John was glad for the mild temperament of the Morgan breed or he'd not have been able to separate her from her foal.

Something Laureate had shown him occurred to John. Though the situation was different—a disjointed hip rather than a clubfoot— the old man's wisdom came back to him.

"Remember, lad, if a bone needs mending, do it as soon as the animal is born and the bone is yet soft."

Bjorn came and handed John what he'd asked for and knelt beside him to help. The foot became noticeably straighter as John continued to massage the ankle and Bjorn put more pressure to turn it. When at last it was aligned just a little beyond where it should be, John took a piece of burlap and wrapped the leg as Bjorn held it in place. Putting the slats of wood on either side of the ankle, he trussed it tightly with twine, wrapping it around and around until nothing but the ends of the slats showed. The foal lay with his eyes rolled back, and John, when he first saw this, thought the small animal had died until he touched the foal's face and the eyes turned to look at him. He didn't want to hurt the foal, but he also knew that had the leg remained disfigured, the colt would have been killed. A horse that could not walk properly was of no value.

The foal soon got to his feet with their help and immediately walked about, neighing softly as he looked for his mother. John brought the mare back to her baby and left them alone.

"That was something, what you did," Bjorn said. "The Captain will be glad."

"If that foot doesn't turn back again he might. Otherwise, he'll think I hurt the poor little critter for nothing."

Not even the events of the evening before, when she'd bathed her brother's face with water and with tears, would cloud her confirmation day. Mary was up earlier than usual, cooking porridge while she waited for the pots of water to heat so she could fill the washtub and take a bath and wash her hair before the others got out of bed. She drew the curtain along the wire stretched across the corner of the kitchen and stepped into the tub. Squatting in the warm water, she sighed blissfully. Then, knowing the others would soon be up, she hurried. By the time little Anna pattered into the room, her night-clothes soaking wet, Mary was drying her thick, shining hair over the heat of the stove.

"Oh, Anna, you've wet yourself again." Mary was glad she'd left the bed she shared with her tiny sister before she'd gotten soaked as well. But not even Anna's bed-wetting, or anything else, was going to put a damper on this day. Mary took the wet clothing from her sister, and scooping Anna into her arms, she placed her in the tub of still-warm water to let her splash and play while she stirred the porridge and called to her brothers.

Frederick shuffled in and pulled a chair from the table. Leaning his elbows on the table, he held his head in his hands and moaned, "Don't want to go on that route no more. I know I have to, but I don't want to."

The others had come in and stood about the table, but the room was quiet, no one knowing what to say. Mary laid a comforting hand on her brother's shoulder. She hated that her brothers had to provide for the family as they did. They were much too young for such hard work, and now, dangerous work. Would the German guards add yet more torment after the events of the night before? Her face flushed in silent anger as she thought of Frederick's humiliation.

It was Lana, as she dressed Anna, who brought everyone back to the day at hand. "Are you forgetting what day this is? It's Mary's confirmation day."

"Ah…Mary, I'm sorry, I forgot." Frederick stood and grabbed Christian's hand and he likewise the hand of Thea, and soon they were all holding hands, with Mary in the middle, as they danced around her until Mary said, laughing, "Stop! Stop! It's time to eat and get on with the day. I will tell you all about it when you come home."

Mary was late to the church. Her classmates were already standing in place in front of the altar, which was draped with the traditional fine white embroidered mantle. Lighted candles illuminated the gold Communion goblet as it stood in readiness. Tanta Dorthea sat among a small audience, a look of anticipation on her face as she turned her head upon hearing the door open and then sighed with relief at seeing her niece.

The heavily carved door shut behind her, and Mary in her new dress walked quickly down the aisle and took her place between Eva Svensen and Olaf Dahl, both of whom smiled angelically as they gave her room. Reverend Pederson cleared his throat and glared at her over the top of his glasses before continuing with the confirmation exercises.

Afterward, coffee and pastries were served and then Mary stood with Tanta Dorthea while receiving congratulations from those present. Reverend Pederson gave everyone in the class a small Bible and as he placed Mary's in her hand he said, "And now, Mary, what will you be doing? Will you consider your Tanta Dorthea's offer? It would be a fine opportunity for all of you."

Mary glanced at her Tanta and then she said to the Reverend, "I haven't had time yet to decide."

"Think about it, child," he said. "The responsibilities are too great for you, and think of Frederick and young Heinrick. The freight yard is no place for them." Then he smiled. "I know you will make the right decision, Mary, and you have been an excellent student. I often wondered when you found the time to study."

Mary knew what he meant by making a right decision—any other would be wrong. She hadn't expected Tanta Dorthea to discuss her proposal with the Reverend, however, and she was not pleased. How could she decide such a thing so quickly?

Tanta Dorthea sensed Mary's frustration. "I'm sorry, Mary," she said. "I only discussed it with the Reverend to get his counsel in the matter. I have no one else to advise me. I didn't know he was going to bring it up on your confirmation day. Will you forgive me?"

Mary's hazel eyes twinkled as she smiled at her Tanta. She had been so kind to her and to her sisters and brothers, but Mary needed time to think. She said, "Thank you for being so kind, but I can't think what is best just now. I will talk to my brothers and sisters. It is they who must decide."

Everyone was full of questions at supper, and Mary told them the events of the day. Keeping her conversation with Reverend Pederson from them, she found it hard to look or feel happy.

It was several days before she had the courage to talk to anyone about Tanta Dorthea's proposal. It was after supper, and both Christian and Anna were asleep in their beds. Thea sat by the hearth, her head resting in her hands and her elbows on her knees. She looked unusually pale, Mary thought, and sent her off to bed as well. She hadn't argued, as she was accustomed to do, but she showed no sign of a fever. The child was probably just tired.

Everyone was busy with one thing or the other as they sat by the table.

Mary watched them for a moment before she said, "We have something to talk about."

All eyes in the room came up to meet hers, and Lana asked, "What is it?"

"It's about Tanta Dorthea." Not knowing how to cushion the matter, Mary took a deep breath. "She wants us to come to live with her." Resting her eyes on Frederick and Heinrick, she said, "She thinks you should give up the coal route."

Frederick grinned. "She does? I'm all for that." Then he said seriously, "But how could we get by?"

"Tanta said you could work about her house and grounds and go to school. She said you all could go to school."

"What of you, Mary? Will you go to school as well?" asked Heinrick.

"*Nei*, I am almost fifteen, and Tanta and the Reverend think I should take a position as a cook's helper or perhaps a seamstress."

There was silence as they contemplated the change in their lives.

Mary would not influence their decision, but she was not at all sure how she wanted it to be. There were things to consider. The horses, for instance—would they be sold? She could hardly think of such a thing. Pa had taken such pride in the dappled team and in the little black-faced cow that had seen them through times when all they had was her rich milk to drink or use for the milk gravy to pour over their boiled potatoes and cabbage. Hadn't they churned butter for the rich pastries that Christian stood on the corner to sell? And what about her promise to Mama to take care of the family? Had she done her duty? She wished Mama could tell her what to do, but then she remembered—it was not her decision.

The little colt's foot healed without a noticeable turn of the ankle, but not without putting pressure to it several more times. The Captain or John would massage the ankle vigorously before applying a new splint. The Captain was pleased with John's quick action after the colt's birth, but having remedies of his own, directed the foot to be placed in a pail of warm salt water for the pressure and massage treatment.

As the Captain and John knelt beside the colt their conversation often turned toward John's childhood and the Captain would ask him about his family.

"You said you have a brother. How old is he?"

"I'm not certain, but I think he is eighteen or twenty. I was small when we were separated."

"Do you know where he is?"

"*Nien*...but I thought I saw him once. I'm not sure that it was him, of course—I was only eight years old and hadn't seen him since I was four—but there was just something about the boy I saw. I only saw him for a few minutes and the next time I looked he was gone."

"Where was that?"

"In town! I unloaded the wagon and was left alone for a while. I was looking down the street at the shops, wishing for a bit of chocolate, when I saw him getting into a wagon. He sat there like he was waiting for someone and I was about to call out to him when Herr Helvig, the man who had my keep, came up behind me and told me to get back to work. Next chance I had to look, he was gone. I told Herr Helvig that I thought I'd seen my brother, but he scoffed, saying I wouldn't know him if I saw him. I suppose he was right...but there was something about him. I couldn't see his face very well...maybe it was the way he moved or maybe his hair. It was dark and wavy like mine. I don't know, sir, I guess it was more...a kind of feeling." John remembered that night so long ago when he'd cried, longing to find his brother, an empty sort of longing as if he were lost forever.

"Feelings that strong are something to heed. What town was it?"

"Moorland, I think. Away up north anyway." His answer was offhanded; John couldn't figure the Captain's interest.

"You never saw him again?" the Captain persisted.

"No."

They both fell silent as they took the colt's leg from the water and bound it tightly to the splint. Then, as if thinking out loud, the Captain said, "I wonder if he was confirmed."

John looked at the Captain but offered no comment.

The summer was soon upon them and John Peter was spending more and more time working the yearlings, breaking them to lead while carrying the weighted burlap bag on their back, all in preparation for the time, as two-year-olds, when they would be broken to both saddle and rider and to the harness.

One day, four of the Captain's two-year-olds were to go to auction and be sold to the highest bidder. John was invited along. Excited about the outing as he was, the thought of losing the four horses into someone else's care dampened his enthusiasm. The bay mare more than the others had been a challenge. The high-spirited filly had fought him every inch of the way, kicking wildly the first time he put the empty burlap bag on her back and tied it with leather straps around her belly. She'd fought the lead as a yearling, fought the saddle, and tried every trick to rid herself of her rider just the month before. But when John finally won the battle, the bay mare tossed her head in the air and then brought it down to nudge him as if to say, "You won, but I gave you a run for your money, didn't I?"

It was not yet noon when the horses were unloaded and led into a holding pen. On the post beside the gate was painted the number 8, meaning that the Captain's horses were eighth in line to enter the arena and be auctioned.

Bjorn was invited to go as well, and the Captain told them their time was their own until his horses turn came up, when they would be needed to lead them about the arena.

On their way to the market square they walked beside the white board fence connecting the holding pens, where elegantly groomed racehorses to shaggy cart ponies whinnied nervously. A team of dappled grays led by two boys approached, followed closely by a smaller boy and four girls. The eldest girl, obviously the one in charge, carried a little girl on her hip. She smiled shyly as they passed, and John and Bjorn smiled and tipped their hats. The matched team was sleek and shiny and their manes hung in many long, thin braids tied at the ends with bits of red yarn. The children had not looked glad to be there and John momentarily wondered why, but then he caught sight of the fairway and all thoughts were lost in their excitement.

"What should we do first?" Bjorn asked.

"My mouth has been watering for a big fat sausage…ah…and I smell smoked fish…that sounds good, too." John breathed deep of the smells of food from the various venders ahead. "What about you?"

"The fat sausages wrapped up in cabbage leaves sound good, but my mouth is craving something sweet and sticky."

John took another deep breath, and then another smell, one not so pleasant, reminded him of the first time he was there. They were passing near the hog pens, and his recollection of the hated farmer invaded his thoughts. He could see his face as clear as if he were standing there before him, right down to the mean, evil glint in his eye.

Bjorn, noticing how quiet and tight-lipped John had become, asked. "What's the matter?"

"I got a whiff of the hog pens and it took me back to my first time here. You know…when I had to duck the farmer so he wouldn't find me. I was craving those fat sausages then, too, but never got a chance at them. I had to get out of here fast." Then, grinning, he said, "It was the same day I took your job."

Laughing, they hurried on and were soon savoring a fat sausage wrapped in cabbage leaves, juice running down their chins. Sticky, sweet *bondepige med slor,* baked layers of honey and breadcrumbs, satisfied their cravings and they leaned back on the wooden bench and belched out loud.

Open booths surrounded the market square, where one could choose his game of chance. Passing the ring toss and dart games, they stopped to test their strength, as first one and then the other lifted the heavy sledgehammer into the air and crashed it down, sending the pounds marker flying up the scale. Though John's blow sent it the farthest, it was not without regret when he felt the leather truss slip above one of the ruptures on his groin. A searing pain sent him to his knees and onto his back. He managed to press the rupture back into place and adjust the truss. Bjorn looked on, alarmed by John's pain and ashen face, until he recovered and got to his feet. His face was red with embarrassment. Returning to the auction he explained his actions to Bjorn. John was strong and capable, but he would struggle with his condition the rest of his life, always relying on the leather truss to keep the ruptures from protruding.

The Captain hailed them from his seat above the arena where he'd been watching the progress of the auction. Joining him, they took a seat as a black gelding was put through his paces in the arena, walked this way and that, mounted, and given commands as the man tightened the reins in one direction and then another.

"It won't be long now before you'll enter the arena. Did you boys have something to eat? I can smell sausage."

But as John began to answer using the Danish word for sausage, the Captain cautioned him with a quick shake of his head and nodded toward two German officers in the row below. Until then, the Captain, being German himself but speaking both German and Danish, had made no mention of the German ordinance forbidding Danish to be spoken.

Bjorn quickly whispered into his ear about the ordinance. "I thought you knew. You were speaking so earlier."

"That was because you were." And than in German he spoke to the Captain.

"I almost forgot…I brought you a sausage." John pulled a sausage, wrapped in a paper soaked with grease, from his pocket. The Captain grimaced at the sight but took it gratefully and ate it in two bites.

Bjorn handed him a crushed sticky parcel; the sweet had fallen apart and was stuck to the wrapper. The Captain declined the thoughtful offer with a smile.

The three went below to ready the horses, and when it was time John led the bay mare into the arena and soon the bidding began. Soon it was over and the bay mare was led away by a stranger.

The Captain's horses brought a good price and he was anxious to collect his money and return home. As they were leaving, they noticed the matched dapple-gray team enter the arena.

Once the decision was made to live with Tanta Dorthea, everything moved so quickly, they could hardly catch their breath. First, the gentle black-faced cow was taken to a small pasture behind their Tanta's gardens and a place in the barn prepared for her shelter. The children's belongings were packed and carted to the big brick house. Soon the dreaded day arrived. They were all going to the horse auction to say good-bye, even little Anna. But first Mary, Lana, and Thea parted the horses' manes in small sections and braided each one. They tied a bit of red yarn at the ends, all the while crooning their regrets for selling them and laying their wet cheeks against the dapple-gray coats.

Frederick was feeling bad enough about having to sell the horses and was getting impatient with his sisters. "Can't we go now?" he growled. "The auction will be over by the time we get there."

Frederick and Heinrick scowled as they led the team toward the auction pens. Their sisters and younger brother followed, holding back their tears. They were directed to number 9 on the far side of the arena.

When their number was called, Heinrick led the mare and Frederick led the gelding into the arena. Moments later, the bidding began. Mary looked up into the stands and saw a German officer raise his hand to bid. She cringed at the thought of their beloved team belonging to someone like the guards who'd tormented Frederick. But then there was a shout from below with a higher bid. The tension mounted as first the officer and then the other bidder shouted out a higher bid. In the end, the German officer stood and, slapping his leg with his gloves, looked about to see who had beaten him with the highest offer, but the team was already being led away. Saddened at the loss of the team, the children's spirits were lifted knowing that the German guards did not have them and that they'd gotten a goodly sum.

Closing up the house where they'd lived as babies in their mother's arms was difficult, and yet, the excitement about living where they would be fed and clothed in a style they were unaccustomed to brought giggles and laughter to the young hearts. Only Mary felt some apprehension at finding a position.

A few days after everyone was settled, Tanta Dorthea asked Mary to come to her room. When Mary entered she asked, "Would you care to have an audience with the retired captain that Reverend Pederson spoke of? He has a position to be filled as soon as possible and the Reverend has already spoken to him about you. However, it is your decision to make."

Mary stood, tight-lipped and pale, afraid to answer. How could she do what was being asked of her? She'd never worked for anyone other than her family and now she was expected to go to a stranger for employment and possibly live in a stranger's house? She was so afraid that her legs felt weak.

"Mary, dear, are you afraid? You look dreadful. We'll just tell the Reverend that it is too soon to make such a decision." But as Tanta Dorthea started for the door, Mary cried out, "Nein! I will go to see this captain. I'll go first thing tomorrow morning."

"Are you sure, Mary?"

"Yes!"

"Would you like me to go with you?"

"No! I'll go." The fear hadn't left her, but an unyielding determination to see it through took hold of Mary.

The next morning, without saying a word to the others, Mary left to find her way to the retired captain's home. The directions took her through town and into the countryside beyond. It was still early when she saw the white fences and the big white house. The dirt track led between the fenced pastures and paddocks to the main house where flowers crowded the walks and porches. At the door, she was asked to wait in a small vestibule for the captain. She looked down at her blue patterned dress and dusty shoes and wondered if she should wipe them off. Catching sight of herself in a mirror attached to a hall tree, she saw her hair sticking out in little wisps from around her cloth hat. As she stood before the mirror, poking them back under her hat, a door opened and a large man with a graying, dark beard entered. Mary's face felt hot as she turned to face him, but he quickly put her at ease.

"Do you wish to start today or do you need time to gather your belongings? I prefer that you live in my house, and I think you'll find the accommodations adequate. You will have ample time to visit your family and they can visit you as well, so long as it does not interfere with your duties."

Mary felt as if she'd been struck dumb until the man smiled at her and she found her voice. "I will need to get my belongings, sir. I should have brought them but I…"

"No need to explain. I will have John take you for them, but first I will take you to Dora. She will instruct you."

Entering the summer kitchen where Dora was shredding cabbage for kraut, the Captain said, "Dora, this is Mary Knutsen. She'll be helping you. She has walked a long way and must be hungry. I'll go for John. He'll take Mary to get her belongings."

When he was gone, Dora placed a hand on a rounded hip. "Mary Knutsen, is it? Where did you work last?"

"I haven't, except for the care of my own family. I've had charge of them since my parents died."

"And now…have you abandoned them?"

"Certainly not." Mary could feel her anger rise at the accusation, but Dora continued.

"Well, Mary Knutsen, the Captain is a fine man to have your hire. He'll treat you good and give you a fair wage so long as you do what's expected and that will be to help me in the kitchen and to milk the cows morning and evening. The Captain likes them milked out in the pasture when the weather permits; otherwise, Bjorn will have them in for you."

Then she smiled and her eyes crinkled almost closed in a round, merry face. "Come on, my girl, let's find something for you to eat and then I'll show you where you'll sleep. John will be along soon to fetch you."

Mary must have shown her amazement at the change, for Dora laughed and said, "You'll get used to me in no time at all."

After a hearty bowl of cabbage soup, swimming with chunks of carrot and ham, and a thick piece of warm bread, Dora showed Mary to a small but comfortable room off the main kitchen. "It's here where you'll sleep and keep your belongings," she said. "It's a good bed, too," she added as she tested its resilience with her hand.

Returning to the summer kitchen they found John standing by the door.

"*Ja*, and it's John to fetch you," Dora explained. "John Adamson, this is our new girl, Mary Knutsen."

John put out his hand and smiled "Pleased to make your acquaintance, Mary. The Captain has instructed me to take you for your belongings. Are you ready to go?"

Mary stood for a moment, puzzling over the young man. Hadn't she seen him before? Then she remembered. He was one of the young men who'd smiled at her at the auction, and she said, "Yes, thank you. I am!" She turned back to Dora. "Thank you for the delicious meal. I'll see you when I return."

After John climbed into the cart seat he gave Mary a hand up and they started off. Dora called after them, "John, you be careful of my new girl." He looked back and nodded.

They were silent for a time, and then John asked, "Aren't you the girl who I saw at the horse auction?"

"*Ja*," Mary said shyly.

"Were those your brothers and sisters?"

"*Ja*. Frederick and Heinrick were leading the horses, and I was carrying Anna. The others were Lena, Thea, and Christian."

"That was a fine-looking team."

"*Ja*, it was a sad day that we had to sell them."

"I could tell...why did you sell them?"

Mary explained about her parents dying and how she'd taken care of the family since then, explaining, "It was not me alone; they all helped. Frederick and Heinrick took over our father coal route, and Lena and Thea helped with everything else. Christian sold the pastries I made at the street corner. Then our Tanta Dorthea offered that the children could live with her while I took a position. That is why we had to sell the team."

"I see."

They fell silent once more. John clucked at the chestnut mare to hurry along and she broke into a trot. Soon they entered the city and the sound of the horse's hooves changed to a clatter on the cobblestone streets.

Mary pointed the way when they drew near the Church of Saint Nicholas, where they were to turn, and said, "It isn't far now." She pointed. "That red brick house is my Tanta Dorthea's. Go there to the side entrance and I will collect my belongings."

When Heinrick and the older girls, who were cleaning weeds from the flowerbeds, saw who had arrived they ran excitedly to Mary, all talking at once. Mary held up a hand in a gesture for quiet and said, "What is this, have you never seen a horse and cart before?" But before they had a chance to answer Mary introduced John and told them she was here to fetch her belongings.

"But, Mary, how far away will you be? We've always been together," Lana wailed.

Heinrick stepped forward and took hold of Lana's sleeve. "Stop your blubbering," he said and then he waited for his sister to explain.

"I've taken a position as cook's helper and milkmaid at Captain Kruger's. John works for him as well. He is the stable boy." Mary could see that her sisters were on the verge of tears. "Don't fret so. I'll see you often," she said bravely. "The Captain said so, and you can come to visit me as well."

At this their faces brightened, yet Thea said as she lowered her eyes, "We'll miss you, Mary."

"I'll miss you, too," she whispered, "but now I must gather my things so we can be on our way." Turning to John, who still sat on the cart, she said, "I'll only be a moment."

"Take your time, we haven't far to go."

Mary, accompanied by her sisters, went inside to see the others and collect her belongings while Heinrick talked with John. "Is this Captain a nice man to work for? I wouldn't want Mary working for a grouch."

"A grouch he is sometimes but never unkind. I'll tell you just how kind he is if you promise not to tell."

"*Ja*, tell me!"

"Remember at the auction, when the German officer and some-one below the stands was bidding on your team?"

"*Ja*. We were glad the German officer didn't get them. We were so afraid that they would end up in the hands of the guards at the freight yards…but how did you know about it? Did Mary tell you?"

John reminded him about passing them at the auction, adding, "We had just left the stands when you and your brother entered the arena with your team. Bjorn and I recognized the team and called them to the Captain's attention. He liked the team right off and bid them away from the German officer."

"You mean our team is at the Captain's, where Mary will be? Can we see them when we visit Mary?"

"I'm sure the Captain won't mind."

"Does Mary know?"

"*Nein*! I haven't told her. The Captain doesn't even know the team belonged to her family."

"She'll be so glad. When will you tell her?"

"I won't. She'll see them for herself when she goes to milk in the morning. I'll make sure they're in the paddock nearest where she'll be milking."

"This is great news," Heinrich said. Just then, Mary, holding little Anna, and the others came toward the cart.

"What's great news?" she asked Heinrick, placing Anna in Lena's arms and reminding her to take good care of her.

"Oh, nothing," said Heinrich. "I was just saying that it's good that the Captain is such a good man as John here has described him."

They waved until John and Mary turned the corner by the church and the chestnut mare trotted out of sight.

Dora was preparing the evening meal when John delivered Mary and her belongings at the kitchen door. Wasting no time, Mary set her things away and returned to help, asking, "Do you want me to do the milking now?"

"*Nein!*" Dora said. "You can begin milking in the morning. Greta will milk today before she leaves. A moment later, a young red-headed woman opened the door to the kitchen and came in. It was obvious that she was expecting a baby, and soon.

"I've come for the milk pail," she said. Then she groaned. "I'm glad there is only one to milk and that she is a considerate soul. I think she knows that I can't move very fast." Noticing Mary, she brightened. "Ah, and this must be Mary! Welcome..."

"Greta is leaving us to have her baby, and then she and her young husband will go to America," said Dora.

"How wonderful to be going to America," Mary said, "and of course it's wonderful that you're having a baby. Are you sure that you can do the milking today? You look..."

"*Ja,*" said Greta, "I know how I look...I'm as big as a house but I am well and feel good, and besides, I must say good-bye to Rona. I've been milking her since she dropped her first calf. Tomorrow you'll have your chance at her, and in a few weeks you'll have two more cows to milk."

Greta left for the pasture and Dora handed Mary a stiff white apron like her own. "Now, Mary Knutsen, my girl, you'll slice the meat and bread for the Captain's table."

"Per, Per…a letter has come!" The young woman stood just outside the doorway of a small stone house, calling to the young dark-headed man coming slowly toward her, but still some distance away. He didn't quicken his steps or acknowledge her prodding. "Come along, Per, don't you hear me? Your footsteps are like a snail's."

Coming closer, Per scowled. "What are you saying?"

"A letter has come for you."

"A letter? Who would send me a letter?" He reached the stoop and took the envelope from his wife.

Per had been more fortunate than John, having accomplished his studies for confirmation; it was only because of this that he held a letter from Captain Kruger of Abenrade in his hand. The Captain had learned the name of John's brother through their conversations and had set about looking through confirmation records until at last he had a lead on John's brother's whereabouts. The letter, however, had gone through many hands before it reached Per Adamson. The Captain's hope of finding Per was unknown to the young man who groomed and trained his horses. The Captain hadn't wanted to raise false hopes.

Carefully opening the envelope, Per unfolded the page and read first to himself and then aloud, his face beaming in an uncontrollable smile.

"Listen to this, Marie!"

To Per Adamson,

Let me explain if you have indeed received this post. I have in my hire a young man by the name of John Peter Adamson. It is from him that I obtained the name of his brother, Per Adamson. It is my hope that you are one and the same. If in truth this is the case, will you tell me by return post so arrangements can be made for a reunion?

Captain J. Kruger

"Per," his wife said, "this is truly an answer to prayer. I know how you've longed to find your brother all these years, and now we know it has been your brother's prayer as well. When will you answer?"

"Now! I'll answer his letter and you can post it in the morning."

Their cottage was sparsely furnished, but Marie's lively blue eyes lent hope, as well as joy, to its character. A table spread with a white cloth was set for supper, which was bubbling in a pot on the black iron stove.

Per sat at the table, clearing a place to write.

To Captain Kruger and my dear brother John Peter,

I read your letter and want to tell you how happy it has made me. I am John Peter's brother and will anxiously await our reunion. I have married, and my wife, Marie, is with child. We have two older children, Peter and Anne. Our home is in the village of Hostrup where I work at a dairy. The German border is almost at our backs. How ironic that we are so close. Can you come to stay with us for a time, John? I await your return post.

Per Adamson

When John and Per were separated, Per had remained in the same place with the uncle he'd been sent to. The uncle lived closer to their father, but Per had seen him only a couple of times and was never allowed to live in his father's home, so Per refused to see him again. He knew their sister as she grew, but Per was never allowed to live in his father's home. After a time, Per refused to accompany his uncle on such visits. Finally, Per's uncle sent him to live with a friend in the southern part of Denmark near the German border. It was here where Per began his studies and was confirmed. It was here, too, where he met and married his wife Marie.

Per was recalling his childhood when Marie interrupted him. "My father's sister lives in Abenrade," she said. "She has often told my mother that they could use a good hand at their dairy."

"Meaning me, I suppose."

"*Ja!*"

"We are Danes," Per said, "and I don't want our baby born where we can't even speak our own language."

"But, Per..."

"Nei!"

Marie knew better than to pursue the matter, so she held her tongue for the time being. Per, however, was not ready to give up defending his stand.

"Wasn't it enough that the German dogs came across our borders and took our land," he said, "without imposing their guttural speech on the people and then taking our potatoes to make the swill they drink?" He was red in the face and beginning to sputter. Marie soothed, "Na, Na...don't go on so. We'll stay right here so you won't have to look at those German dogs, as you call them, but I wonder how your old friend, Hans, from the fodder house would take your slander of his homeland. Would you call Hans a German dog?"

"Nei! Of course not."

"There you have it..."

"Have what?"

"The reason you shouldn't call them German dogs."

"Nei! It's a different matter. Hans lives and works in Denmark. He lives by Danish rule."

Marie couldn't argue with this so instead she said, "Do you think all German soldiers like their role as invaders?"

"*Nei*, but I've heard horror stories about some of the German guards. So have you."

"*Ja*, I have…but still…" Marie could see that it was useless to argue and changed the subject back to the matter at hand.

"I wonder how long before you hear from Captain Kruger or your brother." She wanted to mention that Kruger was a German name, but instead she waited for her husband's reply.

"I don't know, but I hope soon." Per's face broke into a broad grin again. "I'd just about given up hope of ever seeing him again. He was so small when we were separated. I saw our great- uncle once, but he was so feeble he couldn't remember John, let alone where he'd been sent."

Mary had slept far better than she'd anticipated upon slipping beneath the covers of the small bed the night before. She'd lain awake for a time, thinking of her family and of this change in her life, going back and forth as fear and then excitement crept into her thinking, until she fell asleep.

The slightest glow of dawn filtered through the curtains at the small window above her bed, and Mary heard her name spoken. A moment's hesitation brought her mind to focus and she realized that it was Dora, calling her to get up. Mary answered her and dressed quickly in the coarse brown dress she'd brought for doing chores and twisted her hair into a bun at the back of her head. Hurrying into the kitchen, she found Dora standing at the big stove stirring mush while thick bacon sizzled in a black iron pan.

After the morning greetings, Dora pointed with the wooden spoon toward the long table at the side of the room. Several places were already set with bowls and small plates. "Bring your bowl! You'll have time for a bit of breakfast before Bjorn comes for you."

Mary did as she was told, pouring thick cream over her mush and a spoonful of dark sorghum. She'd just finished when the kitchen door opened and a boy of perhaps her own age entered. She recognized him at once as the boy she'd seen with John at the horse auction.

Still half-asleep, he growled, "Are you ready?" Before Mary could answer, Dora glared at the boy and scolded him. "Have you no manners? You haven't been properly introduced and yet you take on such a tone?"

Bjorn's face flushed to the color of his red freckles as Dora introduced the two young people and sent them on their way to milk.

Nearing the pasture, Bjorn said, "Sorry I was so bad-mannered. I didn't mean to be rude."

"I didn't take it that way," Mary said. "It's barely daylight and too early to think about politeness. Besides, I already knew who you were." She told him of seeing him at the auction with John.

A number of cows grazed in the pasture, and Mary asked, "Which one am I to milk?"

"The one there, nearest the fence." Bjorn pointed. "She's easy to milk and doesn't kick. But wait until that black one comes fresh—she's a devil."

Bjorn handed her a small three-legged stool, and Mary patted the cow's rump and sat down by her udder. The milk rang into the blue-and-white-speckled pail as she leaned her head against the cow, feeling her warmth.

When the milking was done, Bjorn took the pail, but before turning toward the house, he called Mary's attention once again to the black cow at the far side of the pasture. It was then that Mary saw the pair of dappled grays in the adjoining paddock. She was so flabbergasted that she could barely speak, for she knew the team at once.

Looking at Bjorn, she said, "Why…what…is it really them?"

"*Ja*, it is."

"But how…? We sold them at the auction!"

"I know," said Bjorn. "The Captain bought them, bid 'em away from that German officer. I'll just set the milk over the fence and then we'll go see them so you can say hello."

As they approached, the mare flicked her ears and whinnied softly, bobbing her head before prancing toward Mary; the gelding followed. Tears ran down her face as they nuzzled her affectionately, and she patted and hugged the beloved team. John watched quietly, unnoticed from the stable door.

Several days passed before Mary had an opportunity to thank the Captain for buying the team. One evening, as Dora and Mary served the hired hands their supper, the Captain walked in holding an envelope. His face did not betray emotion, nor did he reveal his intent, except to say, "John, come around to my study when you've finished supper." Not waiting for a reply, he walked to the door as Mary stepped to his side.

"Captain," she said, "could I have a word with you?"

"What is it, Mary?"

"I want to thank you, for buying our team."

The Captain looked puzzled. "Your team…?"

"*Ja*! The dappled grays at the auction."

"Ah…the dappled team…so they were your family's…I didn't know, but it's a fine team."

When John entered the Captain's study a short time later, he was handed the envelope. Embarrassed, he stared at it, not knowing what to do. Surely the Captain would know he couldn't read…

At that moment, the Captain realized his blunder and took the envelope from John's hand. Withdrawing a folded paper, he opened it and read it aloud. When he finished, he waited for John's response.

"My brother...? How could he know I was here?" The color drained from John's face. What kind of joke was this?

"I located your brother by searching confirmation records," the Captain said. "I knew that if, by chance, he'd been more fortunate than you and been confirmed that I might find him, and as you can see, I did." The Captain didn't wait for a response before he said, "Now we must plan a reunion. Do you wish to go to his home, as he suggests, or, do you want him to come here?"

"I...I don't know," John said. "I can't say...what do you think?" The news was beginning to sink in and what looked like a permanent grin spread across his face.

"Consider!" the Captain said. "If you go to your brother's home, you will be in Danish territory and under Danish rule. I could take you myself, which would lessen the chances of being found as a runaway, but you do not have papers. You were fortunate to have escaped the border patrol when you came here, but, of course, it's easier to come in than to go out. I believe it best that your brother come here. A visitor pass is easily gotten so long as you can prove where you reside. If we had more time, I could arrange for the proper papers for you, but it could take months. I know a few people who owe me a favor or two, but they are in Berlin just now."

John studied the Captain's face in admiration. No one had ever been so kind or cared one way or the other—except for Laureate. Always, he'd been like a lone thistle growing in a pasture...trampled and cursed, but he'd sprung back in spite of them.

The Captain laid a piece of writing paper on his desk and fingered a pen stuck in an inkwell. "What will we tell him?" He waited for John's reply.

"Ask him to come here and tell him why I hesitate to go back across the border, if you will, sir. I'm very grateful for your doing all this for me. I cannot thank you enough."

The Captain took the pen and began to write. When he was finished, he cleared his throat and read:

Dear Per,

I was very glad to receive your post and look forward to seeing you. At this time it would be advisable for you to come to me. I will explain further when I see you. The Captain tells me that you can easily obtain a visitor's pass for a few days. I hope this will be convenient for you. I am so glad to have found you and await your return post.

Your brother, John Peter Adamson

John was excused to go back to the stable, assured that the letter would be posted the next day. But as he opened the door, the Captain said, "John, wait a moment. Would you like to learn to read and write and do numbers?"

Dumbfounded, John said, *"Ja...*I would."

"Good. We'll begin after your brother has been here. You can go now."

This was all too much to swallow at one time. John wanted to talk about it. He wanted to shout about it, but who would listen? Then, as he passed the kitchen door, it opened and Mary stepped out to shake the crumbs from a tablecloth. Her hair hung loose down her back, but the white starched cap kept it away from her face. The Captain must love the look of stiffness, he thought, since Mary and Dora and the housemaids were always clad in the same white starched aprons and caps. Mary's was now soiled from the day's work.

She shook the cloth with a sharp snap and then saw John watching her.

"Oh...you startled me."

"Sorry," he said. "I was just wondering how you could wear all that stiff stuff. Doesn't it get in the way?"

"Sometimes."

"How about when you milk?"

"Oh," she laughed, "I take off the apron when I milk. Goodness, I'm afraid Blacky would kick me right out of the pasture if I tried to milk her with it on."

"Say, I'll bring the team around any time you want," John said. "I was watching you the day you first saw them. I put them in that paddock on purpose. Bjorn was in on it too. I knew how happy you'd be."

"*Ja*…I was so surprised I could barely speak. But I must go inside now. Dora will have something for me to do before bedtime." She turned to go inside and then stopped and turned back to John. "Did you speak with the Captain?"

"*Ja*," he said. "Can I tell you what's happened?"

"Of course," said Mary. "I was afraid I was rude to ask."

"Nein, I was hoping to tell someone. The Captain has found my brother. I haven't seen him since I was four years old. The Captain wrote a letter for me, asking him to come here for a reunion."

"How wonderful! I'm so glad for you."

"*Ja*, and that's not all…the Captain has offered to teach me to read and write and to learn my numbers."

"Oh, John," Mary said, "that is good news. I must go. Until tomorrow then…"

A brisk breeze flapped the laundry as Mary hung the Captain's bedding and table covers on a line to dry. Stopping to poke a loose curl beneath her white starched cap, she saw the Captain walking toward her. "Good morning, sir," she said.

"Good morning. I have a number of errands to attend to in town today. I thought perhaps you'd like to visit your family while I am about my business."

"Oh, sir, I would indeed," said Mary.

Only Thea and Anna were at home when Mary entered the house, and little Anna ran into her arms. The others were in school but for Christian, who'd gone with Tanta Dorthea on an errand.

Hugging her sister, Thea said, "We miss you. It seems strange to live in this big house without you. Tanta is very kind, but she does like it quiet. She gets very nervous at any sort of silliness or banter. I think Christian is her favorite because he's so serious all the time. You know how serious he is."

"I hope you are all behaving," said Mary. "she lets you have time for play, doesn't she?"

"Oh, *Ja*," said Anna. "So long as we're quiet. It's just so different and hard to get used to. I'll be glad when I'm old enough to find a position." Then, remembering the German officer's wife who'd wanted Lana to sew for her, she said, "but not any old German lady."

"Nei, nei, Thea," said Mary. "You must not talk that way. She was really very kind as soon as she understood the reason why Lana could not come into her house to sew."

Then Mary told Thea and Anna about living at the Captain's and about Dora and Bjorn and John Peter, whom they'd already met. She wanted to tell them about their team, but she waited, hoping the others would get back before the Captain came for her. She wanted to see all of their faces light up at once when they learned that the Captain had bought them. But Thea spoiled the surprise when she said, "Do you get to pet Prince and Princess?"

Mary's jaw dropped. "What…how did you know?"

"When John Peter brought you for your belongings, he told Heinrick. He said he was going to surprise you by letting you see them in the paddock when you went to milk."

"He did, did he? Now he's gone and spoiled my surprise. Oh well, the important thing is that they're at the Captain's and not with the German guards. I was so surprised when I saw them that I couldn't speak."

"Do they still have their braids and red yarn?" Thea asked.

"Nei," Mary said, "but they are sleek and well fed. You can see them when you come to visit. When will that be, do you suppose?"

"Tanta Dorthea said we can visit you one day soon."

"Good, I want you to meet Dora. She is teaching me to cook many new things."

"Do you like it there?"

"I miss you all very much, but I do like it at the Captain's. Except for Blacky. She is the most hateful cow I've ever milked."

"Does she kick?" Thea asked.

"*Ja*, she kicks."

Mary smiled at Anna, who had fallen asleep in her arms. "Has Anna stopped wetting the bed?"

"Nei. She wets more than ever, almost every night, but we don't tell Tanta Dorthea. We don't want her to scold Anna."

The Captain came before the others returned, so Mary laid Anna on a settee and said good-bye to Thea. "I'll see you soon then," she said, "give my love to everyone."

It was unsettling for Mary to know that her brothers and sisters were not as happy as they might be. Thea had said they were expected to sit quietly on straight-backed chairs when visitors came, sometimes for hours, but Mary strongly suspected that that was more than a slight exaggeration.

It had been three weeks since Per wrote to his brother, and he was getting impatient for a reply. Every day, he asked the same question: "Has a letter come?" And every day there was no answer, until at last, Marie stood in the yard waving an envelope as he came up the path.

After reading the letter to Marie, Per said, "We'll go as soon as I find someone to take my place at the dairy for a few days."

"I think you should go alone to see your brother this first time, Per," she said.

"Why, Marie? You're my wife."

"I know," she said, "but you will need time to get reacquainted. Wouldn't it be easier if it were just the two of you?"

"Well…," said Per.

"You know it would." And it was settled

The next day, Per made arrangements to be gone for two days and sat down to write his reply to his brother. Two weeks later, a visitor's pass in his pocket, Per mounted a small bay mare and was on his way.

Marie, holding little Anne in her arms with small Peter standing at her side, called after him, "Have a wonderful visit and give John my greetings."

"I will!" he waved.

John was given a cot to put beside his own in preparation for his brother's arrival, and when the day came, he waited nervously. He'd kept busy all morning feeding the horses and turning them out to pasture. He even cleaned the stalls and put down fresh bedding. But now he stood at the side of the stables, watching the drive that led from the main road between the pastures and paddocks to the house.

He was watching so intently that he didn't hear the Captain until he'd come up beside him and spoke.

"He'll be along," he said. "You're watching the road won't bring him any sooner."

The Captain's face wore the closest thing to a grin that John had seen. His manner was usually stern, hiding the gentleness beneath.

At that moment, just as John turned his head toward the Captain, he saw a rider out of the corner of his eye and his head snapped back. "It's him! Here he comes." And he walked quickly to the paddock gate to wait.

The awkwardness they'd both expected was forgotten as Per jumped from his horse and the two embraced, tears in their eyes.

Once Per's horse was fed and watered, the two went in search of the Captain, who'd disappeared.

"I want you to meet him," John said. "I didn't know he was searching for you until your first letter came."

There was no sign of the Captain, however, so they returned to John's quarters until supper. Sitting on the edge of his cot, John was the first to speak.

"Tell me where you've been all these years and about your wife and children…everything."

"I've not a lot to tell," said Per. "I stayed with Uncle until I was fourteen, and then he sent me to stay with a friend until I was confirmed. I never went back. I went to work at a dairy and then later I met Marie and we were married, and now Marie is going to have our third baby." Hesitating, Per said, "What about you, John? I asked our great-uncle about you, but he was so feeble…he didn't know where you'd been sent after his wife died."

"She had me tending geese from the time I was four until she died. I've hated geese ever since. Then I was farmed out to two old men who were bachelor brothers. They didn't like me much and decided I wasn't worth my keep, so another farmer came and got me. He was part-German and had been raised in Germany. He'd had to take over the family farm in Denmark when his father died and wasn't too keen about it, so he expected everyone who worked for him to speak German. He was a spiteful man. I got a few strappings over speaking Danish, I'll tell you. He raised hogs and horses and I was put to work with the hogs. I haven't much use for hogs either, since I was almost killed by a big boar. The stable groom, Laureate, and took me under his wing and persuaded the farmer to let me exercise the horses. He taught me everything I know about horses, and enough German to get by, but then he died and I was sent off again, this time to the worst of the lot. When I was fifteen, I left. I ran as fast and as far as I could, and here I am."

John left out the parts that still gave him nightmares. He felt resentment at having suffered so much when his older brother had obviously had an easy life. His face must have shown this, because Per said, "I'm sorry you had things so rough. If only I'd found you sooner…"

John couldn't help wondering how hard Per had tried to find him. Not wanting to spoil their reunion, however, he asked a different question.

"What do you do at the dairy?"

"Milk."

"How many cows?"

"Twenty, more or less. I'm not crazy about it, but it pays my wage and I'm good at it. I can milk three to the others' two. What do you do?"

"I'm the stable boy," said John. "I feed, water, and exercise the horses. Clean stalls and help when they foal. Say, are you hungry? I think it's about time for supper. According to the rumblings in my stomach anyway."

"I sure am!" said Per.

As they started for the house. Bjorn appeared from the barn and was introduced. "How many cows do you milk, Bjorn?" he asked.

Bjorn shook his head. "Mary does the milking. There are only three cows. The Captain raises beef cattle along with the horses. Though the horses are his pride and joy, right, John?"

John flushed. "I guess so." Per looked puzzled by his reaction.

The table was set and Mary was dishing up steaming bowls of food when they entered. They sat down after the introductions, and Dora filled their cups with hot coffee. Filling Per's, she said, "So, you're John Peter's brother." She studied his face. "There is a likeness, all right. How much older are you?"

"Almost four years."

Per did not hesitate when the food was passed to him, but filled his plate. John was still in the habit of watching how much Bjorn took as a measure to go by.

After supper, back at the stable, Per watched as John led first one and then another prize horse into its stall with a gentle hand and a kind word. He untied a burlap sack weighted with a few pounds of grain from the back of a young filly before leading her into a stall.

Per asked, "What was that?" John explained the technique for early breaking, then, with his back to his brother, he fastened the latch on the stall's door and said, "Have you seen our father and little sister?"

Per cleared his throat. "It's been a long time."

John turned abruptly toward his brother. "You've seen him then? What did he say? Did he say anything about me?"

"Uncle took me to see him a couple of times, but he never talked to me. He acted as if I weren't there. Once I asked if I could come home to live and he said, 'Nei!' It was the only word he ever spoke to me." Per looked down at his feet. "After that I refused to go back. Uncle tried to make excuses for him, but I was having none of it. As for our sister, she's nothing but a chore girl, wiping up after our father's new family. She'll get out of there as soon as she can. I know she will. Whenever I tried to talk to her, Father would send her out of the room. She might have gotten away already…I suppose she's sixteen by now. I'll have to find her."

"Why do you think he sent us away in the first place?"

"The woman he married didn't want us."

"Why did they keep our sister then?"

"She was a baby and I suppose no one wanted her."

"*Ja…*" John sneered, "she was too small to work."

The days passed quickly, but before it was time for Per to return home, the Captain offered him employment so that he and John could be near one another. Per declined the offer graciously. He had no intention of living in an area occupied by Germans, although he had the utmost respect for the Captain.

The day of his departure when Per mounted his horse to leave, Dora came running with two parcels tied together with string to be hung over the horse's saddle. "Here are pastries and sausage for your table. Keep your fingers out of them until you get home." The look she gave him was stern, but her eyes twinkled.

"I'll come to see you when I have the proper papers to cross the border," John said. "Tell Marie I'm anxious to see her."

It was the following spring before the Captain managed to procure papers for John, making him a legal resident of German-occupied Denmark and subject to German rule. He had mixed feelings, as though he'd given away something of himself yet gained a feeling of safety.

It was not a good time to be gone, since several foals were due, but the Captain insisted. "I don't believe we'll need to worry for at least a week and you'll be back by then," he said. John was allowed to pick the horse he would ride. Dora handed him a small parcel, explaining, "This is something for their new baby, and," handing up a cloth bag, "This is something for their table. Keep your fingers out of it."

It was late afternoon by the time John Peter rode up the narrow path to his brother's home. The door swung open at the approaching hoof beats and a young woman holding an infant stepped out. Dismounting, John went up to her and said, "I am…" but she didn't let him finish.

"I know who you are. It's so good to see you, John Peter. This is Louie…" Looking behind her, she said, "And Peter and Anne are hiding behind me." She held the baby out to John to hold. "Go on…he won't bite, you know."

John took the baby carefully and looked into his face. "Louie, you say…that's a fine name. I guess I am his uncle then."

Looking at the two small faces peering out from behind their mother, one on either side, he winked and said with a grin, "I am your uncle as well."

They tittered and hid their faces in their mother's skirt.

"That you are, Uncle John," said Marie.

"Is Per at home or is he milking?"

"He'll be along soon." Taking the baby from him she pointed with a nod toward a small shed. "You can feed and water your horse over there and turn her into pasture. Then come inside."

John was soon sitting at the table with the baby in his arms, the two small ones clinging to his pants legs, their shyness gone as Marie opened the parcel from Dora. Holding up an embroidered coverlet she said, "It's beautiful, almost too beautiful to use." Then she put a dozen or more pastries and a roll of smoked sausage on the table. "How thoughtful," she said.

John was still holding the baby when Per walked into the room. "I see you've met Marie and the children." He beamed.

"A fine family, Per. You're a lucky man."

"Supper will be ready in a few minutes. Go get washed." Marie prodded. "You smell like the cow barns themselves."

After supper as they sat and talked before the fire, John asked, "Have you given any thought to coming to work for the Captain?" Per's face flushed and he could feel Marie's questioning eyes on him.

"Nei! I can't say that I have. I like it here and Marie's folks live near. You are not that far away that we can't visit one another."

"That's true, "said John. "It took me but six hours to ride here, and now that I have papers I don't have to worry about being stopped."

"Do you think they would send you back to that farmer? You're not a boy anymore." Per hesitated. "I was hoping that you might come live with us."

"Thank you, it is good of you to ask," John said. "But I like it where I am, just as you do. The Captain has been kind to me and I like working with the horses."

"*Ja*…I could see that, and you're good at what you do, just as I am good at milking."

John enjoyed the visit, but he was anxious to get back to his horses. Worried that one might foal without him, he cut his visit a day short.

"I'll come back later this summer if I can," he said. "The Captain told me to tell you that if you ever want to visit, he'll make room for Marie and the children in the house. I wish you could—Mary and Dora would love to get their hands on Louie."

The next two months were busy anticipating which mare would foal next. When a chestnut mare came walking in from the pasture with a foal at her side, the same mare they thought still had a few weeks to go. Bjorn said, "Can you beat that? You expect that with cows but not horses."

John laughed. "I guess it happens—there's the proof." The Captain came up behind them wearing a rare grin. "Where do you think horses had their foals before there were stables or barns?"

Well into the season, John was looking over the mares yet to foal when he noticed that Princess was showing all the signs of having her foal soon. The Captain was anxiously awaiting the foal, hoping it would resemble its sire. The sire was a dapple-gray Clydesdale stallion from the next district, and the Captain had been waiting anxiously for a sign. The Clydesdale was known for his fine stance and was sought after, along with his mate, to lead many honored processions. John hurried to find the Captain, who followed him back to the stable.

Princess snorted and bobbed her head when John and the Captain entered her stall. Without speaking, the Captain examined the mare, and then turned to John. "We'll be having a foal by morning," he said. "Go have your supper and than come tend to the mare. I'll spell you in a few hours. Get Bjorn to stay with you if you like."

Bjorn and John took turns napping as they watched and waited for the inevitable change in the mare's condition. By two o'clock the following morning, they knew it would not be long. Bjorn was about to start for the Captain when he appeared. Two hours later, a foal stood nursing at his mother's udder. He wore the same white star on his forehead as his mother, but it was there the likeness ended. He had the large flared feet of a Clydesdale and the uncomely short, thick neck of his father's breed.

The Captain's pleasure was plain to see.

Hours, and then days, passed with Mary rarely in the kitchen. She had been put to knitting when it was learned that she could do so, and aptly. It seemed everyone was in need of new socks and leggings. The Captain was no exception, adding a vest to his list.

There were still the cows to milk and the washing to be done but Mary no longer had to fear being kicked by the hateful black cow. The cow appeared on their table in the form of succulent roasts and fragrant meat pies, and Mary felt no remorse.

The months eventually became years. Mary turned twenty in a wink of an eye, as Dora put it, and each time she saw her family she was startled to see their growth. Little Anna was learning to sew, but she remained pale and small for her age. Thea had taken a position in a house about which Mary felt a sense of foreboding. There was something in her sister's manner that disturbed her, but Thea denied any problems, and Tanta Dorthea seemed perfectly happy with the arrangement. Lana had long since taken over the duties of Tanta Dorthea's housekeeper and was pleased with her lot. Christian was nearly as tall as Heinrick, his thick blond hair adding perhaps an inch, and his blue, twinkling eyes endeared him to anyone he met. He was nearing completion of his confirmation classes and was hoping to continue his education. Heinrick was still the serious, kind rewarder of praise and he was still watching out for the entire family. At eighteen, Frederick had become a man. Tall and broad with dark hair like their father's and the disposition of their father's brother Nels—quick to anger and quick to make amends—a constant worry to Mary was that at any moment he could be forced into the German army.

Mary frequently accompanied Dora to the Church of Saint Nicholas, where she had been baptized and confirmed. Reverend Pederson had retired and in his place was Reverend Shultz from Berlin. A nice enough minister were he not German, Dora pointed out, back in the Captain's kitchen. Speaking in the forbidden Danish she said, "Nei, it's not like our own *Sct Nikolai Kirke* Saint Nicholas."

Mary did not disagree and yet she said, "*Ja*, our schools are in the hands of the Germans, and they are taking our young men to serve in their armies and now they have taken our church, but...the Captain...he is German."

"*Ja*...the Captain is German," Dora said. "But he has lived here many years. He made his home here when it was our sovereign Denmark. When I first came to work for him we conversed in Danish because he spoke both and I spoke little German. He is a shrewd man...kind, but shrewd. He'll keep John Peter and Bjorn from the German army. Just wait and see."

Mary was silent, but in her heart she thought of Frederick and Heinrick and Christian, her beloved brothers.

The Captain had acquired a mail route, and since John had more than satisfied his expectations in learning to read and write, he offered John the job of carrying the mail.

It had been a year since then, and John went each morning, wearing the uniform of a mail carrier and driving a dapple-gray team as he sat beneath a shroud at the front of the covered mail wagon. It had taken him some time to get comfortable in the heavy uniform with its shining brass buttons, and especially the awkward plumed helmet, but despite it all, it was a prestigious position for someone of his background and he was grateful for the opportunity.

Little time was spent at the Captain's—leaving at dawn after an early breakfast and back shortly before the evening meal, he had little opportunity for conversation with Bjorn or Dora or even the Captain, but he found that he missed Mary's company the most.

There were Sundays, of course, when he did not go on his route, but on Sundays, as well as after supper during the week, he was kept busy with his stable duties. One Sunday, after the Captain had sold a number of horses at auction and John had little to do, he went in search of Mary. He found her coming from the milk house with a large pitcher of milk in her hands. When he spoke, it startled her, and some of the milk slopped over the side onto her apron. Her face flushed. "Oh my, John," she said. "You startled me."

John's face turned crimson too. "I'm sorry, Mary, but I've been looking for you. Do you have time to talk?"

As John took the heavy pitcher from her, Mary's face flushed again. She wanted to talk with John as much as he wanted to talk to her. They'd seen little of each other for so long. She would just have to forgo going with Dora to church.

"I usually accompany Dora to church on Sunday mornings," she said. "But I don't think she would mind if I missed this once." She didn't tell him what Dora had said, that she'd seen sparks fly between them whenever they looked at one another at meal time, it being the only time they saw each other for any length of time. Just the thought of Dora's words made her face burn the more.

At the kitchen door Mary took the pitcher from John and hurried inside, saying, "I'll meet you at the garden bench in a few minutes."

But John had a better plan.

"The Captain said I could take the buggy for the afternoon if you'd like to take a ride."

"I would," said Mary. "I'll be ready when you come for me."

Dora was ready to tease the moment the door closed. "*Ja*, and just where is the young man taking you, Miss Mary?" Her eyes twinkled.

"We're going for a buggy ride so we can talk. May I be excused to change into my Sunday dress?"

Dora merely nodded and waved her hand, feigning irritation, but her eyes smiled.

A short time later John Peter handed Mary up into the buggy seat and they were off. The Captain and Dora stood by the garden gate watching them go.

They were silent until they reached the main road. Then John asked, "Where would you like to go?"

"I don't care, John," Mary said. "This is lovely."

"Well, then," he said, "we'll go to the park and have a picnic." He pointed to a basket on the seat beside him. "Dora packed us a picnic lunch. There are some of those juicy sausages and I don't know what else. Would you like that?"

"*Ja*," said Mary, "that would be very nice."

When they reached the park, they spread a blanket on the grass and opened the basket. By this time, they were deep in conversation. Mary was careful not to drip the juice from her sausage on her dress and ate daintily, while John made no pretense of manners, wiping his hand across his mouth and then on his pants leg, until he caught Mary's eye and apologized for his manners.

"How far must you go on your route?" she asked as he took the last bite of his sweet potato.

"The route is the outlying parts of this district. I come to the mail station here in Abenrade and collect the mail and at the end of the day I bring the mail I have collected on my route into the mail station and my day's work is done. Then I go home and eat supper and look at you."

"Look at me? Why do you look at me?"

"Because I still cannot imagine how you can work or do anything with all that stiff stuff on. Besides, it gives me pleasure to look at you."

Mary's face felt hot and she knew it must be red. Ignoring his last remark she laughed, "Well, what about you, in that heavy uniform and your plumed hat?"

"It's not a hat! It's a helmet," he scolded.

"It looks like a hat to me," she teased.

"Say, how is your family?" John asked. "I haven't seen any of them for some time."

Mary's look became serious. "They are well."

"You don't look as if you really believe that. Is something wrong?"

"That's just it, I don't know. It's Thea...I just feel something is wrong at the house where she works. Tanta Dorthea says they are very nice and respectable people and Thea confirms it, but..."

"Thea would tell you if there was something wrong."

"*Ja*, I suppose she would. She's always confided in me before."

"There, you see..."

"Where the others are concerned, Anna is still pale and too small for her age, but she has started school and Lana is teaching her to stitch a sampler...Christian is almost as tall as Heinrick and he's almost finished with his confirmation classes... Heinrick is still looking after everybody else and Lana is Tanta Dorthea's housekeeper. That leaves Frederick, who I am most concerned about."

"Why is that?"

"Because I know he could be forced into the German army, and with his temper..."

"Mary, don't worry so much. When it comes to things you can't control you just have to push it out of your mind."

"Push it out of my mind?" she said. "Frederick is my brother."

"I'm sorry," John said. "I only meant that...well...when you hate a thing so much that you can't think about it without boiling up inside, when the hate scares you, all you can do is push it away. Get it out of your mind so you don't have to think about it."

"John, I don't hate anybody. But I do worry about my family some times and the thought of Frederick or Heinrick being taken into the German army." Mary covered her face with her hands and said, "But there is nothing I can do about it." Then she straightened and rested her hands in her lap. Looking at John, she said, "It must have been terrible for you—all those years of being sent from one place to another, not even knowing why your father sent you away." Mary knew the hate he had spoken of was his own that caused him such pain.

"I hate him, Mary," said John. I hate the places where I was sent and I hate the farmer at the last farm the most. But, as I said, I have to keep it pushed away and try not to think about it."

But Mary knew that even though he tried not to think about those years, it was always present. She could see it in his eyes at supper when he must be comparing the fine meal he was eating with a bowl of watery, cooked cabbage and a slice of stale bread.

"Oh, John, it must have been awful for you…all those years."

After riding for a time in silence, John reined the bay mare to a stop and turned to Mary. "I didn't mean to spout off like that," he said. "I wanted today to be our day. I miss talking to you, but what I really miss is being near you."

"I miss you as well, John Peter Adamson."

"May I court you, Mary Knudsen?"

"*Ja*…you may, but when will that be, John Peter?"

John grinned. "I'll find a way."

When he confided his intentions concerning Mary to the Captain, unknowingly seeking his approval, the Captain felt privileged and awarded John every Sunday afternoon to spend with Mary. They often spent this time with Mary's family, and it was after one of these visits that John asked Mary to be his wife.

The afternoon had concluded in the vestibule of Tanta Dorthea's house as John and Mary were leaving. All but Thea were present when Frederick asked the question on everyone's mind.

Clearing his throat and puffing out his chest in an absurd manner he said, "Since I am the oldest brother, I think it is my duty to ask your intentions toward my sister."

Mary would have crawled under the nearest chair had John not taken her hand and said, "Why, I'm hoping that Mary will consent to be my wife, if I have your permission, sir."

Everyone was excited and bursting with questions. John pulled Mary aside and whispered in her ear, "I hadn't planned it just like this, but will you be my wife?"

Tears swelled in Mary's eyes as she nodded up at him. "*Ja*...I will."

As fall approached, their usual Sunday buggy rides were often altered to having coffee and cakes in the corner of the kitchen under Dora's watchful eye. Fall was a busy time of year, and neither John nor Mary could be spared for a whole afternoon. It was slaughtering time, which meant sausage making and the curing of meat, a preparation time for the coming winter.

The date had been set for their wedding, November 14, 1884. Mary had turned 21 on August 24, 1883, and John would soon be 24 on January 27, 1885, just two months after their wedding.

Preparations were being carried out at Tanta Dorthea's. Lana was busy making alterations to their mother's wedding dress for Mary. Frederick, Heinrick, and Christian were making a serviceable cart for the couple, and Anna was stitching a sampler for their parlor wall, wherever that would be.

It had come to the Captain's attention that John and Mary would need a place to live. They certainly could not live in John's quarters in the stable or in Mary's small room near the kitchen. But since they were both staying in his employ they would need to live nearby. The thought had occurred to him to give them one of the wings surrounding a small inner court of his house, but when he'd confided the thought to Dora she had heartily disapproved, saying, "They need a place of their own, where Mary can cook her own suppers and, in time, mind her babies."

He found two places available, one of which was a small white-brick cottage belonging to the dairy adjacent to the Captain's. The thatched roof was in a deplorable state and, the Captain ventured to guess, leaking. But when he mentioned it, John was immediately interested, saying how he could restore it to a place Mary would like. When the two went to look at it Mary was less enthusiastic until John convinced her of its possibilities and she conceded. John and Bjorn started to work on the cottage, spending every free moment on it. When Mary's brothers learned of it, they, too, came to help.

Tanta Dorthea had taken it upon herself to make the necessary arrangements for the church and she was gathering together items of furniture for the couple's cottage.

One morning, when Mary came in from milking Dora handed her a parcel. "This, my girl," she said, "is for your wedding. I've been saving them for something special."

Mary opened the parcel carefully and lifted out a beautiful porcelain dog and then its mate from the wrapping.

"They are beautiful. Thank you, Dora. I'll always cherish them. You have always been so kind to me, and one day I will name one of my children after you."

Dora flushed. "Nei," she said, "you mustn't do that." But Mary knew the idea thrilled the older woman's heart.

The day of John and Mary's wedding was cold and blustery. Heavy, gray clouds hung low and one would have thought it might snow, but instead it drizzled a cold rain.

The cart Mary's brothers had made was ready for the occasion, painted blue with red trim and embellished in white chrysanthemums. A dappled Clydesdale was harnessed and standing in wait for the young couple, his mane in tiny braids tied with bits of red yarn.

It was not a long ceremony. The vows were spoken in German, much to Per's chagrin, but bright fall flowers adorned the pews and altar, and John and Mary were dressed in the traditional Danish wedding clothes.

Tanta Dorthea's tables were spread with the traditional wedding smorgasbord: plates of succulent meats accompanied by pickled beets, cucumber salad, caramel potatoes, and red cabbage, along with all kinds of pastries and fruit pudding with cream.

The wedding party arrived, including the German reverend, though he stayed but a short time. He seemed surprised and pleased when Tanta Dorthea handed him a basket of Danish pastries and other food from the table.

When the festivities were over, the party followed John and Mary to their new home. A clay jar filled with beer was set in the middle of a small courtyard beside the cottage, and John and Mary joined hands over it. Frederick stepped forward and smashed the jar into fragments. The pieces were then picked up by the girls of marriageable age. The girl with the largest piece was the one said to marry first. Little Anna, who had been allowed to join in the fun, had the largest piece, bringing rolls of laughter.

Per, Marie, and the children were invited to stay the night at Tanta Dorthea's before going back across the border in the morning. The two families had become friends and stayed up late in conversation. Per, reflecting on his and Marie's wedding, said, "Our wedding festivities lasted for days. I thought they'd never be done with."

Lana added knowingly, "That's a country wedding for you, not like in the city where everything is a rush."

"Ah, but that's not how it used to be," said Tanta Dorthea. "Your mother and father lived in the city, but their wedding festivities went on for days."

Thea left soon after they returned from John and Mary's cottage, with the excuse that she was needed to watch the children when their parents were out.

"Why, Thea, I had hoped you could stay for a while. We seldom see you," said Heinrick.

Lana added, "Why don't you move back to us and forget that position? There are others to be had that are not so demanding."

Thea's face got red, her anger growing—why were they always telling her what to do? Then she remembered that she was in the presence of John's brother and sister-in-law and she apologized.

"I'm sorry that I have to go," she said, "but it was my fault for not informing my employer of Mary's wedding in time for them to change their plans." Turning to Heinrick she said sheepishly, "I'll come home more often, I promise."

The day after John and Mary's wedding was a holiday and there was no mail delivery. The Captain had given them the day off as well, but very early in the morning loud singing awoke them. Family and friends stood beneath their window, serenading them with jocular songs about the forthcoming trials of marriage for the husband.

John, who had given Mary a set of traditional wooden clappers once used to beat clothes washed in a stream—a symbol of good fortune and happiness to the marriage—took them and began clapping them together from the window. The serenade concluded and everyone left with shouts of cheer.

A few more months passed, bringing winter full upon them. Mary was with child, but she was determined to keep her position at the Captain's until spring. Two of the cows were dry, so milking was not that bad. The weather being colder and wetter than usual allowed for her to milk in the barn, for which she was grateful. Knitting and sewing for the men took most of the rest of her time, but by mid-February she had a small pile of tiny embroidered and knitted baby clothes.

One day when she came in from milking Dora blurted, "Look at you, my girl. Your hands and ankles are swollen…even your face."

"I know! I feel awful. What does it mean?"

"It means that you're retaining water. You've got toxemia and that isn't good for you or the baby. I'm putting you to bed in your little room for the rest of the day. You need to keep those feet up and not eat any salt."

"My work," said Mary, "I must do the milking and…"

But Dora said, "Nei! You will do no such thing. Bjorn will do the milking."

By the end of the week, Mary's swelling had gone down considerably, and she planned to return to her and John's cottage, but she went into labor quite unexpectedly. When the baby was born, they named her Mary Inga, after her mother and grandmother. The baby was so small and frail, they feared for her, but in no time at all she began to thrive.

One evening, after supper, Mary sat absently tracing the outline of an embroidered flower on the tablecloth with her fingertip. John studied her for a moment before asking, "What is it Mary? You're so quiet."

"I've been thinking about Anna," she said. "When I see our Mary Inga doing so well I think of how Anna suffered when Mama and Pa died. She was so small and needed them."

"I'm sure you did your best," John said. "I see how she clings to you whenever you're together."

"That's just it. I'm really the only mama she can remember and now she sees me with our Mary, and…"

"What do you want," John said, "for her to live with us?"

"I would like that very much, John," said Mary.

John was silent for a time, his head buried in his hands. Mary could see those bitter thoughts of himself as a child creep over him and she wondered if he would always carry the effects of it. At least little Anna hadn't been abandoned by her family. Mary was about to withdraw her wish when John threw back his head as if flinging the thoughts of himself aside and grinned.

"When can she come?"

"I haven't asked her yet. Are you sure you don't mind? It would mean another mouth to feed."

"Are you trying to talk me out of it? It is settled…Anna comes to live with us."

Mary went to stand behind his chair. She placed her arms around him and kissed his neck. "Thank you, John," she said.

Heinrick brought Anna the following week and as he carried her belongings into the cottage, he motioned Mary aside. "You should have seen how happy she's been since you asked her to live with you," he said. "She's like a new girl! And John…he doesn't mind?"

"Nei," Mary said. "Not at all."

When Heinrick left, Anna came and stood by Mary as she peeled potatoes for supper. Lifting her face, Mary saw there were tears in her eyes and then Anna snuggled her head against her older sister.

"Anna, why are you crying?"

"I don't know," she said. But Mary knew, and she hugged her closer.

The summer was hot and busy and Mary still helped out at the Captain's when she could. Anna proved to be a big help, especially when Mary gave birth to a son, Peter, that fall, although no more was expected of her than they expected of their own children.

Late fall was not only the time for butchering and all that accompanied it; it was also time for harvesting the vegetable crop. The Captain's store for the winter was kept beneath the kitchen in a cool cellar, but since John and Mary had to use another method, having no cellar, holes were dug the width and length of a man's arm and as deep as was necessary to prevent the frost from reaching the contents. Straw was laid in the bottom, and then the vegetable digging began. First, potatoes were dug and put in the hole, adding a layer of straw every so often, with a thick layer on top and then two thick rounds of peat. As many holes as were needed to house the potato crop were dug and filled, before doing the same for the turnips, rutabagas, beets, and cabbages, although they used far more straw for them. Kale kept well in the garden, weathering the first frosts. A cold frame was then laid over the holes to keep them as dry as possible.

Mary and Anna dug the holes while Mary Inga and Peter carried the straw, shrieking with laughter as they ran back and forth and then helped to fill the holes. They were delighted at their father's praise when he was told how hard they'd worked.

Mary Inga followed Anna everywhere. She helped her in the garden and held the yarn between her small, outstretched hands as Anna wound yarn balls.

Peter waited for John to come home from his route each day, anxious to accompany him to the Captain's while he attended the horses, squealing with delight when he was lifted to the more gentle horses' backs as John exercised them in the paddock or rode with him about the pasture.

Mary was expecting their third child now and was too busy to go to the Captain's except on special occasions, such as when the lard was rendered or the sausages made. Her wage for this was a portion for her family, which Dora amply supplied. The dark blood sausage encased in the scraped and cleaned intestines of the butchered animal was boiled in water. Many foot-long sausages two or more inches in diameter were boiled in a large iron kettle over an outdoor fire. Other sausages were prepared in a similar manner or left for hours in a slow oven. The remainder of the meat was cut up and laid in salted layers in a stone crock for later use or fried and laid down with hot grease to seal each layer, a generous amount of grease poured over the last layer that filled the crock.

In the spring, a German method of preserving the old hens that no longer laid eggs was used. The drawn hen was hung by its feet in the ceiling above the large, black stove, where it grew sour and stinking long before it was dried, and was then laid away to be used in a German stew, a stew that would never pass Mary's lips. Mary could scarcely stomach the smell of the drying hens under normal conditions, but being with child made it worse. More than once she'd had to find a place to vomit.

The spring that year was particularly wet and cruel. Cold winds cut across the flat lands in gale force, entering every crevice of the cottage, which was rapidly growing too small for the growing family. The howling wind ruthlessly ripped up sections of fence, throwing them hard against the cottage.

Mary bent over a table kneading bread dough while Peter stood, nose pressed against the window, anxiously watching for his father. Anna sat cross-legged on a bed shoved against the kitchen wall with little Mary, teaching her to stitch.

It was growing dark and the wind continued to howl. John was late, as was expected in such a storm, but supper could wait. Time went by with no sign of him, and finally Mary fed the children and put them to bed. Anna waited with Mary until she could hold her eyes open no longer and she, too, went to bed.

Some hours later Anna heard Mary call softly, "Anna, my time has come, I don't want to send you on such a night but will you go to the Captain's for Dora?"

"*Ja*! I'll not be long," Anna said, hurrying into her coat.

"Follow the fence," said Mary. "Don't lose sight of it! Yell into the barn for Bjorn and he'll take you the rest of the way."

Outside, the storm still raged, the sky black as pitch one moment and then suddenly illuminated by a yellow moon, which swiftly disappeared as black clouds were blown across its face, leaving an eerie green silhouette.

Her hand skimming the rail as she hurried, Anna followed the fence to the Captain's. At the paddock gate leading to the barn she hesitated, feeling suddenly very alone. At the barn she called and her voice cracked nervously.

"Bjorn…are you there?"

After a moment he answered, voice sleepy, "*Ja*…who is it?"

"It's me, Anna… I must get Dora. It's Mary's time."

The next minute Bjorn was by her side pulling on his coat. "Where's John? Why didn't he come for Dora?"

"He's not come home. Mary is awfully worried," said Anna. "And now it's time for the baby. She told me to hurry. She said you'd go the last way with me. It's so dark."

"Come on! Here, hold my hand," he said as he led her toward the big house.

Dora was up and dressed and heading for the door almost before Anna could catch her breath. She, too, asked, "Where's John? You shouldn't be out on a night like this." When told that he hadn't arrived home she clucked her tongue against the roof of her mouth and hurried out into the storm to Mary.

When the three came to the cottage, Mary was in great distress. Dora sent Bjorn to tell the Captain about John's absence, but no sooner had he gone than John appeared at the door.

"Where have you been?" Dora scolded. John only scowled at her as he removed his coat and hung it on a peg to dry. He was about to ask why she was in his house at that hour when the sound of Mary's labor silenced him.

"It'll be awhile yet," said Dora. "You'd best go to the Captain so he knows you are safe. I'll tell Mary you are home."

John put his coat back on and went again into the night.

At the Captain's, he told him why he had been so late, first assuring the Captain that his horses were safe. "A barn collapsed and fell across the road. If I'd been a hair faster, it would have come down right on top of us. Prince has a scratch on his side from some flying glass or something, but he's fine. I couldn't get around the wreck so I went back to Kristen Olsen's. He offered his barn to shelter the horses in until I can come for them. The mail cart is inside as well."

Then, seeing the stricken look on the Captain's face, he said, "I'm sorry. I didn't know what else to do and the wind was fierce."

"Nein, nein," said the Captain. "The horses are in good hands, but what about you? Did you walk all that way home in this storm? What happened to your face?"

"My face…?" John, touching it, brought his hand away with drying blood on his fingers. "I must have caught some flying glass myself. No matter, I'd better get back home. Mary is…"

"*Ja*…you'll be having a new one soon but you'll be needing something to warm you before you go," said the Captain. "Besides, you will only be in the way until it is done."

It was well into the morning before Anna came to fetch him. The storm was over and her face was aglow with the news. Finding John peering from the stable door, she announced, "John, come home. The baby has come and it's a girl."

The tiny baby was named Dora Amelia Tora. She lay in Mary's arms, and while her family clearly adored her, Dora felt a certain pride she'd never known in her little name sake.

Frederick had long since reestablished his father's coal route when he found working about Tanta Dorthea's grounds unsatisfying.

The German guards had not changed, still watching to make sure that he took no more coal than his orders called for. Their manner towards him, however, had changed. They now merely growled at him and walked away instead of harassing him as they had when he was a boy.

Frederick bought a fine matched pair of sorrels for the route. The young team was strong with gentle dispositions, and he couldn't help naming them Prince and Princess. On the route Frederick often noticed a young woman hanging clothes to dry in a yard or playing with two small children. He wanted to speak to her, but was afraid, not knowing her place in her family.

One day, an opportunity presented itself when there was no one else about and he needed directions for unloading the coal.

"Pardon me," he said to her, "but could you tell me where to put the coal? The bin is full."

The young woman smiled, showing strong white teeth. Reaching to smooth a wisp of flaxen hair from her face, she said, "Why, I don't know exactly. My father will be home soon, but if you cannot wait you can put the sacks next to the bin and get the empty ones next week."

As she spoke, Frederick was trying to think of a way to learn if she was married and living with her parents with her children or if they were her siblings. She didn't look old enough to have two small children, but what did he know?

When the little girl smiled up at him, he said, "*Ja*, I'll get my sacks next week." And then he blurted, "Are these your children?"

"Mine?" the woman said. "Oh dear me…nei! They are my sister and brother." Then her face turned serious. "Do I look old enough to have two children as old as these?"

Now Frederick was truly in a spot. How would he get out of it without making it worse?

"Nein, nein," he said. "I was merely trying to find out if you are married. I didn't mean that you looked that old."

The broad smile returned to her face. "My name is Elsie, and you are Frederick. I've heard my father speak your name. Next week then…" She turned and hurried into the house, pulling the children after her.

The week dragged by for Frederick until he saw Elsie again, and then a whirlwind romance began. Within six months they were married. Frederick found a small place with three rooms and a place for the horses. While Elsie put her artistry to work turning the rooms into a home, Frederick readied a garden space in a side yard. It was May and early enough for planting.

Elsie had had some nurse's training working in the hospital in Abenrade and she pleaded with Frederick to allow her to continue this work. At last, he agreed. Until they started a family she could nurse at the hospital while he was on his route.

One Sunday, Frederick and Elsie mounted the horses, riding bareback into the country to visit John and Mary. After sharing supper with them, Elsie helped with the dishes and then sat in the rocker, holding little Dora while she and Mary visited.

"I am surprised that Frederick allows you to work at the hospital," Mary said. "He is so strong-willed."

"Oh, I know," said Elsie. "It took me a while to convince him. As you know, he's got these ideas about women working after they're married. It will be only until we start a family, and that may be sooner than he thinks."

"You mean…?" Mary said.

"I don't know for sure, but…" Elsie shrugged her shoulders and grinned.

Mary liked her sister-in-law and thought she was good for Frederick. Never moody or disagreeable, she was able to persuade him from his inclination towards flying off the handle, especially when it concerned the occupying force in their country. Frederick literally hated the German hand on their lives.

Later, as Frederick and Elsie rode for home, Elsie mentioned an observation she had made of little Dora. "She is so pale and has a rattle in her chest," she said. "The other children are rosy and healthy. I didn't want to say anything, but I think she should be seen by a doctor."

"Mary has said as much," said Frederick. "But one day, little Dora is as you saw her and then will have days, or even weeks, at a time when she seems to be well and happy. If you still feel that way when you see her again, you should tell Mary. You are a nurse and Mary is not."

"*Ja*, I will." But the next time the baby seemed healthy enough, and Elsie put her concern aside.

Per and Marie and the children came to John and Mary's in August for a visit and to see the new baby. Mary had planned a smorgasbord of open-face sandwiches for which she'd spent hours readying the many fillings and garnishes. It was to be a family gathering since Tanta Dorthea, Heinrick, Christian, and Lana, along with Frederick and Elsie, would be there. Thea had been invited but no word had yet come from her. The Captain, who rarely accepted invitations, had nonetheless been invited as well, as were Bjorn, Dora, and Signa, the new milkmaid. Even sour old Gilda, the house maid, was included, though no one expected her to acknowledge the invitation since she was used to working in some of the plushest houses in Berlin, according to her.

Dora insisted on bringing the *rodgrod med flode*—fruit pudding—and Tanta Dorthea was bringing the little cream cakes and pastries. Lana made the favored *aebleskiver*—the Danish pastry with an apple filling.

It was late morning on the awaited day when Per turned his mare through John and Mary's gate and the festivities began. First everyone ooed and aahed over baby Dora, and then Mary, Marie, and Anna set to work spreading the tables that had been dragged to the courtyard with freshly ironed tablecloths. By the time the others began to arrive, they were ready to receive them and the party began. Everyone ate until they were stuffed. The sandwiches disappeared with groans of delight, and then the pastries and cakes were set out beside little dishes of fruit pudding and thick cream.

When they were all done eating—at least for now—Bjorn pulled his mouth organ from his pocket and set their feet to dancing. At the height of the merriment Mary happened to glance toward the gatepost, where she saw someone crouched almost out of sight. Without calling attention to herself she went toward the figure and found Thea, her face wet with tears and streaked with dust from the road.

"Oh my dear Thea," she said. "What has happened to you? Why are you crying here by yourself?"

Between sobs Thea said, "Mary I am so ashamed."

"Ashamed of what?" Then Mary received her answer as Thea moved slightly, and Mary could see that her sister was with child. "Who has done this?" she asked. "Oh my poor Thea."

"I am to blame," Thea said. But her crying kept Mary from understanding what else she was saying. She led Thea to the opposite side of the cottage and into the peat shed where they sat on a stack of peat squares. When Thea told Mary that the man of the household where she worked was responsible, Mary asked, "How long has this been going on?" Thea didn't answer, but Mary guessed the truth. She said, "He has been abusing you since you went there, hasn't he? That is why you have been acting so strange and withdrawn. Why didn't you tell me? Why didn't you leave?"

"He told his wife, my mistress, that he will never bother me again, and she has asked me to stay while he is away."

"Away…?

"*Ja*, he left and will be gone for several months."

Mary was angry for her sister. "I see! How convenient for him! Surely you don't intend to stay in that house?"

"Where else should I go?"

"Here! You can stay here!"

"Mary," Thea said, "I can't do that. Besides, you barely have room for your own family and Anna."

"All right then," Mary said. "You can stay with Tanta Dorthea. She will take care of you."

"No, Mary, I'll stay where I am," said Thea. "My mistress has forgiven me. She is really very kind."

"Forgiven you?" Mary's face turned crimson with anger. "Forgiven you? It is not you who needs to be forgiven, Thea"

"I've got to go now," Thea said. "I thought I could face everyone, but I just can't."

"When will I see you?" asked Mary. "How will I know if you are well?" They cried in one another's arms until Thea rose to go.

"Thea, wait," said Mary. "Let me get John to take you. It's a long way and you must be hungry."

"No! I'll send word if I need you. I promise."

"Wait here while I get you something to eat at least." When Thea started to protest, Mary's voice became stern. "Thea, wait! You need something to eat. I'll only be a moment."

When Mary returned to the peat shed she handed her sister a napkin filled with food. Thea hugged her sister once more, went to the road, and was gone.

When Mary rejoined the others John came to her side and asked, "I saw you go into the peat shed with Thea. What's the matter?"

"She's gone," Mary said. "I asked her to wait, to let you take her, but she said no. I think she was too ashamed to have you see her. John…Thea is with child. Her mistress' husband is responsible." Tears sprang into her eyes but she quickly turned aside and wiped them with her apron. "Let's not tell anyone until Per and Marie have gone."

"*Ja,*" John said, "it would spoil everyone's good time to learn such troublesome news." Then, putting his hands about her waist, and with hers on his shoulders, they joined the crowd of dancers as they danced the *var-suvian*, a dance Mary had recently taught her husband. Leaning to her ear he whispered, "Don't worry, we'll care for her."

But that was not to be. Thea remained in the household of her assailant and her mistress for sometime after the birth of her baby, who was named Dorthea.

John and Mary and the children had promised to visit Per and Marie the first part of September, before the crop harvest and butchering began. The warm nights would make it possible for the older children to sleep outdoors. Little Dora and Sena, Per and Marie's new baby, played together in the house. Mary Inga and Peter were excited at the thought of sleeping outside with their cousins, who were always good for a fine time. Anna had chosen to stay at home since she and Lana were planning a visit to Thea.

At the border John pulled out his papers. Pointing out their destination to the guard, he glanced up at the driver of a wagon full of hog crates coming across the border from the north. In an instant he recognized the eyes of the farmer he'd run away from so long before. The man had a puzzled expression as if he should know John, but the guard gave John the go-ahead at that moment and John did something he ordinarily did not do. He slapped the bay he was driving hard across the rump and was over the border in an instant. Mary looked at his ashen face; his jaw set tight and beads of sweat on his forehead.

"It was the farmer, wasn't it?" she asked.

John looked straight ahead and said, "*Ja!*" and they spoke of it no more.

At Per's they were greeted with exciting news.

"John, Marie, can you guess what's happened?" Per said. Not giving them a chance to guess, he went on. "Our uncle who went to America some years ago has sent me tickets to come to his farm in Iowa…in America. Can you believe my good fortune?"

John embraced his brother before saying, "I'm glad for you if that is what you want to do." Then he grinned and said, not entirely joking, "Good fortune must be your middle name. When will you go?"

"Uncle wrote and said we should leave as early in the spring as we can book passage for. He said that way we will arrive in Iowa early enough to help with some of the planting."

"What do they plant in Iowa?"

"Corn and wheat, I think," Per said. "I've been doing some asking and it sounds like they raise hogs in Iowa too."

The women went into the cottage, where Marie told Mary of her misgivings about leaving Denmark and all that was familiar and dear to her. "What if I should never see my family again?" She wept.

Mary put her arms around Marie and holding her, she whispered, "You will, Marie, you will."

During this same time, the Captain used his influence to get Heinrick a job in a creamery in a district to the south. He drove a milk wagon from dairy to dairy, picking up milk cans and bringing them back to the creamery.

A German family by the name of Ewald owned the creamery. Nickolas Ewald had three daughters and two sons. A year after taking the job Heinrick married the middle daughter, Helga. Tanta Dorthea and Lana were displeased with his choice for a wife since she was German and not Danish, but in time she was accepted.

The girl's mother insisted on having the traditional German wedding, and it was at the wedding that Heinrick introduced Anna to his new brother-in-law, Sophus Ewald. Anna was now seventeen, and the attraction between the two was immediately apparent. Mary was strongly aware of the young man's arrogance and his obvious pride in being German and the "conqueror."

Helga, on the other hand, was soft-spoken and unassuming, and Mary knew that Heinrick had chosen well. He would care for her as he'd cared for the family, only more.

The days grew shorter as the last of the sausages were laid away in the cool of the cellar beneath the main kitchen of the Captain's house. The crocks were full, and all was ready for the winter to come.

Weary after dividing her days between helping at the Captain's and harvesting the crop at home, Mary was glad for Anna's help knitting new socks and darning old ones. She managed to find an hour here or there to knit a small cap or stitch a quilt for the new baby growing inside her. This baby would come sometime in the spring, in May perhaps, a good time of the year.

John was busy, too, training a group of yearlings the Captain had purchased at auction. Unfamiliar with John's early practice with the burlap bag on their backs, they bucked and fought his lead at every turn. That, along with his mail route, put him into a gray mood a lot of the time. One night after a particularly difficult day John flew off the handle at Mary when little Dora kept coughing each time he was almost asleep.

"Can't you do something?" he said. "Why is she coughing like that?"

Mary held the baby over a pot of boiling water until the steam loosened her congestion and eased her cough. Mary placed Dora into her little bed and watched until she was asleep. Night after night, little Dora coughed, growing more pale and listless each day. When Mary took her to Dora, the cook immediately sent for Bjorn to take them to the doctor in Abenrade, who determined that little Dora had tuberculosis.

John and Mary were devastated. There was nothing to be done but pray, and perhaps take her to another climate. Desperate, they went to the Captain, who offered to send Mary and little Dora further inland or to the south of France for an extended stay, leaving John and the older children at home.

"How can I do this, John?" Mary asked. "We would be so far from home. I couldn't take a position and care for Dora as well, and what of you and the children? And here I am with a baby yet unborn. There must be another way."

John buried his head in his hands. "There must be something…something we can do…our poor little Dora," he said. "I feel worthless as a father to do nothing."

"John, please…don't," Mary said. "You're a good father. It's not your fault that Dora has been stricken with such a thing."

Lifting his head and straightening his back, John said, "Where did the tuberculosis come from? I thought it was contagious, but I don't know of anyone who has it."

"I thought as you did, but the doctor said it is an unpredictable disease. He doesn't know how she might have been infected. Mary Inga and Peter must be tested too even though neither has a sign of a cough and they are both well."

"Is there no hope if she remains in this climate?"

"There is always hope, John," said Mary. "We must keep praying for God to heal her."

"You speak of God," he said. "What kind of God lets children like little Dora get this sickness? And why does he let them die?"

"Oh, John," said Mary, "we can't blame God. He didn't make her sick, but if it's His will she'll live."

Little Dora was getting steadily worse when Per, who had planned a visit, sent word telling them about Louie breaking his leg and that it was not mending as it should. *We will delay our visit until his leg has mended*, he wrote. But two months later they received another post.

We must delay our visit still as Louie's leg is not mending. We have written to Uncle that we will be delayed coming to America. He has told us to give the tickets to you. He wants you to leave as soon as possible if you choose to go. It is already nearing the end of February. Will you go? I am enclosing the tickets for America for you, your wife, and your four children."

When the second post arrived, John burst through the door with the news.

"We're going to America, we're going to America."

"What are you saying, John?" said Mary. "How can we go to America?" John handed her Per's letter. "Read this."

She looked up from the letter into his face, eyes shining. Her mouth spread into a wide grin and then she said, "Can it be true, John? Are we really going? Oh little Dora...now you can be well again."

Handing her the tickets, John said, "There are so many things to do and so little time. The tickets are for a ship leaving Copenhagen. We must contact the Danish Thiensvalla Line to find out when we can go. How can I do that? I know—I'll ask the Captain."

"Calm down, John," said Mary. "You'll be a nervous wreck by the time we leave. Let's see…how long do we have? It's the end of February…we must ask for passage by this time next month. That would give us a few weeks to be ready."

At the Captain's, John waited for him to read Per's letter and look at the tickets.

The Captain was not an emotional man yet, he spoke with a slight tremor in his voice. "Write to the ship line and tell them the numbers that are stamped on the tickets and ask for the earliest sailing date possible. It is unfortunate you could not go on a German line. You would not have so far to go. You'll need to travel to Sonderborg by wagon, taking only what you know you will need. The ship line will likely send a list of necessities for the voyage itself. Then you'll have to ferry to Copenhagen, where you'll leave your horse and wagon. Hopefully, someone will buy them from you. If you were leaving from a German port, I would take you myself, but since you are leaving from Copenhagen, we'll have to do as we must."

"I wish that were possible," said John. "But since it isn't, we'll have to do as we must. Thank you for your help, and I hope you will find someone to take my place. You've been very kind to me and my family."

Two weeks passed without a word from the ship line in Copenhagen, but it was an eventful two weeks. Mary prepared for the journey with Dora's help, packing the necessary clothing for each family member. When she asked Anna for the clothing she would need, it was not entirely a surprise when Anna told her of her plans to remain since she was going to marry Sophus Ewald.

"I'm sorry, Mary," she said. "I know you wanted me to go with you, but you understand why I can't? I only wish the wedding could be before you leave, but there isn't enough time."

"I understand," Mary said. "But are you sure about your feelings for Sophus? I would hate to leave and find that you'd had second thoughts."

Mary had overheard Sophus say to Anna, "Stop whining. Do all Danish girls whine as you do? If we're to see any more of one another you've got to be more obedient. If I were your husband would you continue to whine whenever you didn't get your own way?"

And now Anna was thinking to marry this man? Mary listened while Anna defended her decision.

"I'm certain," she said. "Sophus says we will live with his parents and help with the dairy and the creamery. He says that he wants lots of children and that we can name one of the girls, if we have girls, after you."

Prompted by an impulse Mary said sarcastically, "Yes, well, if that's what Sophus says…"

Mary stopped herself and softened her next words. "Please write to me, Anna, so I know how you are."

"I will, I promise," she said. "Sophus says that we may go to America as well…in time."

Shortly after this Mary had an unexpected caller.

She hadn't seen her sister Thea for some time and was preparing herself for a visit to the home where she worked when Thea appeared, carrying her child on one hip.

"Thea, come in, come in," Mary said. "I was just thinking to visit you." Reaching for little Dorthea and pulling out a chair for Thea, she continued, "You look tired, Thea, are you all right?"

"No! I'm not," said Thea. "I must leave my position. My mistress' husband has broken his promise. I heard that Anna is getting married and I was wondering if I could go with you to America. Tanta Dorthea has agreed to give me the fare for my little Dorthea's ticket."

"I'll ask John," said Mary, "but I'm certain he will agree. Stay here until he comes home and we'll ask him."

When John came home he was surprised to see Thea and little Dorthea, and was even more surprised at the turn of events, but he welcomed Thea on their trip to America.

Finally, on March 12, the confirmation of their passage arrived from the ship line. It left them little time for last-minute preparations and good-byes. Then, four days before their departure to Copenhagen, a terrible blow fell, when Thea learned that she could not take little Dorthea to America.

Unwed mothers had no say in the matter of their children and since her mistress and her husband, Dorthea's father, wanted the child in their keep, Thea had no choice but to ask to return to their house to be near Dorthea. The man's wife refused her request, blaming her for luring her husband's affections

Thea pleaded with her, giving every reason she could think of to stay in their employ and be with her two-year-old daughter. But it was to no avail. She was turned away without so much as an embrace for her baby, the child screaming wildly, trying to free herself from the woman who held her as the heavy door was slammed in Thea's face.

Unable to face the future without her child, Thea ran wildly from the house, tears streaming down her face. When she reached Tanta Dorthea's door she banged on it for admittance. The hour was late, but soon she heard the latch fall away and Lena opened the door.

"Thea! What is the matter?" Lana asked as she pulled her sister inside.

"They have my baby," she sobbed. "I...I couldn't even hug her or hold her or. Oh, Lena, what am I to do?"

"Who has Dorthea? What are you talking about?"

"My mistress." Thea managed to tell her sister the story. "I can never see her again," she said, breaking down once more into a torrent of tears.

Tanta Dorthea heard the commotion and came downstairs. Seeing Thea's state she rushed to her side in an attempt to comfort her sobbing niece, but upon hearing the cause of her distress, she said, "We'll see about that. Don't worry, my dear, we'll straighten this out tomorrow. For now, you need to rest."

"But, Tanta…how?" asked Thea.

"Never mind what that woman said. They cannot keep you from your baby. I'll look into it in the morning."

Lana led Thea to bed where they snuggled together beneath the covers, but it was near morning before Thea fell into an exhausted sleep.

The morning that had been full of promise, however, dealt one disappointment after another. What Thea's mistress had said was true and there was nothing to do about it short of stealing the baby away from them, which was being strongly considered. Together the family tried to work out a solution to the problem, covering every avenue without success. John and Mary enlisted the Captain's help, but even he could do nothing and time was running short. Thea had two options: stay in Abenrade to be near her child, who she could not see or touch, or go to America, putting that great distance between them with the thought that one day when her child was grown Thea could send for her. Mary wondered how Thea could make such a choice.

Thea decided to go with them to America after Tanta Dorthea promised to pursue the matter. Once the situation was corrected, she herself would bring the child to America or send Thea the fare to return.

The cart built for their wedding those eight years before was loaded with essentials for the journey to Copenhagen and for their voyage across the vast ocean to America and on still further to a place called Iowa. Though the air was warm for March, the family wore their warmest of coats to save space in their luggage.

Dora had packed a large basket of food for the journey and tucked extra sausages in wherever a little space remained. The Captain and Tanta Dorthea gave them money amounting to two hundred American dollars.

Saying good-bye to their sisters and brothers was the hardest part of leaving, and for Thea it was the hardest thing a mother could do to leave her child.

A stop at Per and Marie's across the German border was a welcome relief. It gave them a chance to reassess their load and to make seating more comfortable. Marie suggested hanging two valises on the sides of the cart to make more room, and Per insisted they spend the night and get a fresh start in the morning. Mary and the children were glad of the opportunity, although John fussed about the delay. They were glad that Louie's leg was growing stronger, although he still walked with a stick and a limp.

John and Per sat up late discussing and planning the easiest, if not the shortest, route John would take to arrive in Copenhagen on the appointed date. John wondered aloud why they had to arrive four days before sailing. Per explained, "They told me there were forms to complete and physical examinations and all sorts of things to be attended to before you can board the ship."

"Physical examinations," John said, "Are you certain?" John was instantly put on alert. How could they possibly let anyone examine his small daughter? They would be denied passage if they learned of her tuberculosis. "Little Dora...I cannot let anyone examine her."

"Because of the tuberculosis?" Per said. "But she looks so well.

Much better than she did a couple of months ago. Don't you think so?"

John leaned back and ran his hands through his hair. With his eyes closed he said, "You should hear her...sometimes she coughs so hard she can scarcely breathe. Other times, like now, she is quite good; but it seldom lasts more than a few days." Then, standing up suddenly, John said, "We will have to hope...that is all we can do."

Per agreed. "*Ja*, we will hope she stays well. We will pray."

In the morning, Peter, Thea, and Mary Inga climbed into the back seat of the cart while John helped Mary and little Dora into the front and then climbed up beside them. Waving and hollering their last good-byes, they began the first leg of their journey.

They had gone only a short way when little Dora began to cough. John was quiet, unable to tell Mary what lay ahead in Copenhagen. It was some distance before they came to the road to Sonderborg where they would board a ferry boat to take them around the Isles and across the channels to Copenhagen. John felt like he was retracing the miles he had walked those years before when he'd run away from the farmer. He recalled the farmer's face when they crossed the border to visit his brother's home just a few months ago. A much older face, to be sure, but the same cold, unyielding eyes were there, the same crooked sneer.

"John... John..." Mary shook him to get his attention.

"*Ja*, what is it?"

"You were a long way away," she said. "What were you thinking? If you hold the lines any tighter they'll surely break apart." Mary teased him, trying to force a smile to his grim face.

"I was just remembering the last time I traveled this road," John said.

"*Ja*, I thought so."

Straightening from his slouched position he said, "I'm hungry.

Why don't we stop to eat? There is a good wide place where the road turns off to Sonderborg where we can walk about."

Everyone agreed to the idea.

Mary opened the basket Dora packed for them. Thea and the children held out their cups to be filled with fresh, sweet milk, while John and Mary drank cold coffee from a jar.

The next hours passed slowly, with Thea trying to interest Mary and Peter in a word game. They named things they saw at the side of the road and the others tried to guess what object they were thinking of. When Peter guessed an object in German, the most familiar language he knew, John corrected him by saying the same word in Danish.

"We are in Denmark now and we'll speak Danish. It is our home-land and we will speak our native tongue."

"But, Father, it's easier to speak German," Mary Inga said. "It's what we almost always speak."

Mary quickly admonished their daughter. "Mary Inga, you must not speak that way to your far. We will all try to speak Danish and soon it will become easy. Is that not right?"

Everyone responded reluctantly, "We will do our best." But it proved to be a trying task for all of them, including John, always slipping into German when a Danish word could not be brought up from memory to explain something.

Thea then reminded them, "Soon we will be learning to speak English."

"*Ja*," said John. "That we will. I only wish we knew how to speak it now."

Mary sighed. "*Ja*, it would make it so much easier when we land in our new country. I have heard that it is very difficult when you do not know what they are asking of you, but we will see." When she saw the worried look on John's face, she said, "But I have also heard that there are people who speak your language to help, so I guess we needn't worry."

It was already dusk and there was still a long way to go before reaching Sonderborg. A grassy patch at the side of the road where a small stream passed provided them with a place to stop for the night. While Thea and the children prepared a somewhat comfortable resting place beneath the cart Mary put together a hurried supper. Soon it would be dark. After John unharnessed the mare and led her to the stream to drink he rubbed her down, looking for signs where the harness may have rubbed her sore. When the others crawled beneath the cart to sleep, John pulled up his collar and dozed against a bundle of clothing as he waited for morning.

The next day, they arrived in Sonderborg, where they learned that the ferry had departed some hours before. There was nothing to do but wait until the following day. They repeated the previous night's sleeping arrangements and ate a cold supper while they waited.

It was late morning the following day before the ferry docked and began taking on passengers. There were a number of walk-on passengers, who boarded first, and then the wagons and carts, of which some, John suspected, were also going to Copenhagen to achieve the same purpose as they.

On board the cart was secured with wooden cleats wedged beneath the wheels and the mare was tied to a rail. John and Mary and the children went inside a small cabin with the other passengers. John took a seat where he could watch their outfit from a window, worried that the mare might spook.

When the ferry got to the open channel, where the currents were swift and not cooperative of the way in which the vessel had to go, the ferry rocked considerably for a time and John, never having been on a vessel of any kind, felt queasy, almost to the point of vomiting but he said nothing. The horses were agitated, including John's mare, and were as glad to come to land as he, he was sure.

Copenhagen loomed before them as the ferry came into the slip and docked. It was larger than any city they had seen, having always lived in the country and near smaller towns.

"Which way do we go?" Mary asked, once their cart had reached the street.

"I wish I knew," said John.

Just then a constable stepped to the side of the cart and asked, "Where do you want to go?"

"We are going to America," John said. "We are to go to the Immigrant Hotel. Can you tell us how to get there?"

"To be sure," said the man, giving them directions.

It was late in the day when they arrived at the hotel, and John was anxious to sell the mare and cart. Two uniformed men came forward and directed them to a side alley, explaining that they would help John unload their belongings onto a large wagon. When John protested, he was assured that their belongings would be safe until their departure. But he was told to take whatever luggage they would need during their stay at the hotel.

Concerned, John asked one of the men, "What about my mare and cart? I will need to sell them."

"*Ja*, of course," said the man. "You will have plenty of time to do so tomorrow. In the meantime your horse will be put in the corral and fed."

When Mary asked about the food they'd brought she was told that while at the hotel they would be furnished with meals. So they took what was needed and were shown to a desk to register. But before they were shown to their room a woman came forward and looked through their hair, whispering in Mary's ear, "I am sorry, but I must do this." Mary nodded and smiled. "*Ja*, I know."

The room was small, containing two beds, a table, and two chairs. A water closet was found down a long narrow hallway, a facility that was used immediately by first one and then another of the family. Another family they recognized from the ferry stood waiting for their turn.

Retuning to the room Mary Inga asked her mother, "Why did that woman look at our hair when we came into the hotel, Ma?"

"She was looking to see if any of us have lice," said Mary.

"What are lice?"

"Tiny bugs. But don't worry, we do not have them."

Before they could catch their breath the supper bell sounded and they were ushered to a large dining hall where a plate of food was set before each of them.

The beds were a welcome comfort and they slept until a loud bell sounded in the early morning. Frightened, little Dora cried, initiating a coughing spell. John grimaced at the sound. What would he do if their passage were denied? They would go home, of course, but would it spoil little Dora's chance of recovery?

After a hurried breakfast the family, along with others, was seated on a long wooden bench in a dimly lit, narrow hallway to wait for the examiner. Not the medical examiner, as John supposed, but a person to ask questions. It seemed like hours before they were called into a room with yet another bench on which they were told to sit for another wait. Then, one by one, John, Mary, and Thea were called to a desk where they were asked where they were born, their date of birth, their father's name, their destination in America, who was their sponsor—the questions went on and on—had they ever been in a prison or work camp, did they have any kind of communicable disease or any condition that would prevent them from working. The same questions were asked of John regarding his children, and when he was asked about any communicable diseases, he said there were none. He hadn't wanted to lie, but what else could he do? If his lie was discovered during the medical exam...what then?

Once the questions were asked they were excused, and John learned it was not yet noon. He lost no time taking the mare from the corral and hitching her to the cart. He drove to the front of the hotel and found other men with their wagons or carts, horses, or mules already lined along the curb, waiting for someone to buy their conveyance and animals.

Pulling in behind a sorry-looking wagon with two scrawny mules hitched to it, John swung down and went to stand by the mare's head. Stroking her face he spoke softly, "I wish I could take you with me, girl, but you know I can't. Besides, you wouldn't like it on the ship. I'm not any too sure that I'll like it, either—that ferry trip didn't set to well with me."

As he waited, several men of questionable character walked down the line looking at first one and then another man's outfit, offering small sums only to watch the owners shake their heads in disgust. But as the day wore on many accepted the pittance and watched as their outfit was driven away.

John was ready to give up himself and take what he could get when a man who he'd observed for some time standing across the way walked briskly up to him, tipped his hat, and offered a fair price, considering the circumstances. John accepted the offer and the man said pleasantly, "A fine mare and well trained. She'll have a good home with me." John thanked him and watched as the mare was driven slowly away.

Supper was much the same as the day before—palatable, some of it even good—but a skimpy fare nonetheless. Mary wished she'd tucked some flat bro and pastries inside her valise to share in their room. Others, she noticed, had done that, why hadn't she?

The following day they sat and waited once again—this time for the medical examination—and once again they were called in order, John, Mary, and Thea.

John had not worn the leather truss and hoped his ruptures would not be too conspicuous. The doctor looked at his eyes, ears, and throat and listened to his lungs and then passed him on. Mary and Thea's examinations were much the same as John's except that it was evident that Mary was with child and they asked when the child was due to be born.

John and Mary were then asked to bring their children forward. Leaving Dora with Thea to be examined last, they stepped forward, but when Mary Inga and Peter's examinations were complete the family was dismissed. No one asked to examine little Dora who was sleeping quietly in Thea's arms. Mary started to remind them of her other child until John nudged her and in a low voice said, "Nein."

Later, in their room, Mary reminded him of their deception. "It wasn't right, John," she said. "We should have told them we had another child. It would have been all right."

"All right?" said John. "What if they had examined her and turned us away?"

"We would have gone home and continued to pray," said Mary.

That evening was the last night before boarding the ship, and they were surprised with a traditional Danish smorgasbord. No one knew what food to expect from the ship's galley once they were on board. There was constant speculation about what would happen once they set foot upon the vessel, having heard the tales of those who'd gone before. Some stories were dismal, while others had raved about the hearty meals and almost luxurious accommodations. Their wait ended the very next morning when, after breakfast, they were hur-ried onto wagons fit with benches on either side, along with their baggage and American trucks, a term for the trunks packed thought-fully with the essentials to start their new lives in America.

The wagons rattled over the cobbled streets toward the docks where the ship that would take them to America waited. As they approached they could see

Norge, the name of the ship, painted in large red letters on its side.

On board the steerage passengers were directed to a steep iron stairway. At the bottom, two young Norwegian men stood waiting to lend a hand. Reaching for the luggage handed down to them from halfway up the stairs, they set it aside and reached for more. Step-ping from the last step, John and Mary gathered their family close about them and looked at one another in dismay at the deplorable accommodations. They had been given a piece of paper with the number 3 written on it, a number they were to look for tacked to the bulkhead.

When Peter spotted the number he cried out, "There it is, Father, there it is."

"Nein!" John said. "This cannot be where we must stay."

"Looking at the number, Mary said, "*Ja*, this is it."

Thea stepped before Mary and handed her a paper that had been given to her. A 10 was written on it. "What does this mean; must I find this number and be away from you?"

Mary looked at John. "Surely this cannot be," she said. Then she asked Thea, "What were you told when you were given the paper?"

"To find this number," Thea whimpered, near tears.

John took her arm and said, "I will go with you to find this num-ber and see what it is all about. Leave your things here."

As John and Thea made their way among other passengers who

were also not in the least happy about the living conditions, the number 10 was found at the end of the corridor. Ten obviously referred to the number of bunks fastened to the wall in that area.

Thea buried her face in her hands and said in a muffled voice, "There are men there on some of the bunks. I cannot stay here."

"Nein!" said John. "You will stay with us, your family." And they fled back to Mary and the children only to find another dilemma: there were only three narrow bunks stacked and fastened to the wall. The 3 on the paper had meant just that. A rough wooden table sat in front of them with two short benches, and that was all. There was nothing to give them privacy aside from a partition at either end, and there was little space. What was worse for John at least was the smell of vomit. Although it was clear the floors had been washed, the odor from previous voyages still clung to the wooden planks. His stomach had been a bit squeamish at times, but until the ferry voyage he hadn't known to what extent. John decided to put it from his mind and not think about it—maybe then he could overcome and ward off the results.

Not knowing what John was feeling, Mary said, "We will have to make the best of it. Thea, you and Mary Inga can have the top bunk. Dora and I will take the second." She looked at John. "You and Peter can have the bottom bunk. It's a good thing we all have our own quilt, which will give us two quilts for a bed to keep us nice and warm."

Just then Dora announced that she needed to use a toilet. Mary looked questioningly at John.

"I don't know," he said. "Let me find out...wait here." When he returned carrying a covered bale-handled pail to use as a chamber pot, Dora had tears running down her face and her black stockings were wet and sagging. Trying to comfort her daughter as she pulled off the wet garments, Mary asked John. "What took you so long?"

"I think everyone on board was looking for something," he said, "toilet pails, extra straw bed ticks, drinking water, information. Some were rude—crowding into line, shouting…"

"Oh, Ma, I want to go home," Mary Inga said as she burst into tears.

"Me too!" Peter's lower lip quivered and his eyes were full of tears.

John's patience was wearing thin, but Mary laid a hand on his arm.

"This is a hard day for all of us," she said. "Things will look better tomorrow."

Without comment John left the small, three-sided cubicle that would be their home for many days. A few minutes later the thrust of the ship's steam engines were heard and the ship creaked as it slipped away from the dock toward the open sea.

John reappeared. "Hurry!" he said. "We are underway. We must say good-bye to our homeland."

They struggled up the stairs and joined others gathering at the railing. Some were waving, some were crying, and others shouted things like, "Good-bye my homeland. I will return." For everyone it was a day of sadness, a day of anticipation and hope, and for many a time of apprehension, even fear, as they left their homeland behind.

Peter stayed on deck with his father while the others went below to spread the quilts over the narrow straw ticks. Then they piled their belongings on the two top bunks, leaving the lower one for little Dora to nap. John had retrieved some of the food they'd brought from home, and the basket was set on the table to be eaten from only at midday. They would be served two meals a day from the ship's galley.

Mary Inga sat by little Dora, telling her a favorite story about a little mermaid, while their mother and Thea talked of how they pictured America. Suddenly, Thea lost control of her guarded composure and began sobbing hysterically.

"I should not have left my baby," she sobbed. "I should have found a way. I should have stolen her away."

Mary pulled her close and patted her back. "Oh, Thea," she said. "I know how hard it is for you. When we get to the uncle's in Iowa, if you want, we will find a way to send you back."

Thea sat up straight and was wiping the tears from her face with the back of her hand when John, with Peter in tow, came to a bench and sat down. Oblivious to the scene, he placed his elbows on his knees and closed his eyes, resting his head in his hands. Mary walked to his side and put her hand on his shoulder.

"Are you all right?" she asked.

"*Ja*," he said. But Mary wondered…he was too pale.

It was mid-afternoon when a bell clanged and a voice spoke from a loudspeaker somewhere. The voice was methodical and distinct.

"First galley call…first class passengers, please take your assigned seats in the galley dining area. Steerage passengers, please wait in your quarters to be called."

After what seemed like hours the bell clanged again and the same voice as before announced, "Steerage passengers, take your place in line at the galley door to be served. The plate, bowl, cup, and utensils you receive will serve you the rest of the voyage. A barrel of seawater stands ready where you will wash them. Take them with you to your quarters for the next meal. There will be two meals served a day, in the morning and late afternoon. There are two coal-burning stoves in steerage that are attended to by a ship's steward on which you are permitted to cook coffee. You must provide your own grounds. You will find fresh water on deck for drinking and coffee. Fresh water must not be used for bathing or cleaning. All waste pails must be covered and dumped overboard daily. There will be no smoking, I repeat, no smoking below decks at any time.

This includes pipes and cigars."

The announcement went on and on while families left their areas to climb the steep, narrow stairs. At the galley they were each handed a tin plate with fish balls, boiled potato, creamed kale, and a piece of dark bread. Little Dora was handed a small cup of milk, while the others dipped water from a barrel.

John led the way to a bare table. The white cloth had been removed after its first-class diners had left. There were not enough tables for everyone in steerage, even after sharing. Many sat on benches while their youngsters knelt on the floor, using the bench as a table.

After only a few bites of food John left the table and went back to his bunk. Waves of nausea overwhelmed him, but he managed not to throw up.

As the days passed it became more and more crowded in steerage. Rope clotheslines were strung everywhere. The clothes that were hung on them to dry had been washed in salt water, which left them stiff and gritty-feeling, with a peculiar smell. Mary shook their dried clothes vigorously in an attempt to soften them but it did little good.

April on the open sea was cold, without a sun to warm the deck, and into the end of the first week an oppressive, cold, and heavy mist held the ship in its grasp. Though the sea had been comparatively calm, by the evening of the seventh day the ship broke free of the heavy cover into a torrent of rain with swells lashing at her sides.

John was overcome with seasickness. Nothing would stay down, and at last he refused to eat and grew weaker and weaker.

There were others, too. People moaned and gagged until finally even those claiming strong stomachs were getting seasick. Mary and Thea escaped with few ill affects, and it seemed not to bother little Dora or Peter in the least. Mary Inga suffered, but not as badly as her father.

Mary, and even John in his weakened condition, had been noticing the change in little Dora.

"She is hardly coughing," Mary said, "and see how she runs after Peter."

John agreed. "*Ja*, she is stronger…not so pale.

"*Ja*," said Mary, "now if only you would get well."

John closed his eyes. "How long will it be until we reach America?"

"Only a few days now," said Mary. "And then we will stand on dry land and you can get well."

Mary knew the Lord had heard her prayer when the seas turned calm and the skies cleared the next day, but even with the calming of the ocean people were listless and out of sorts. All around them children cried and mothers scolded. Everyone on board, and especially those in steerage, were more than ready for the voyage to come to an end. Arguments broke out constantly, sometimes ending in a fistfight or harsh, unforgettable words. And the stench…

Then one night, a young man, ignoring the warnings, lit a cigar while he sat on the edge of his bunk. Smelling the cigar smoke, a ship's steward approached. In his attempt to hide the obvious, the young man inadvertently caught his straw tick on fire. As flames leaped up behind him, he insisted emphatically that he had not been smoking. The man and his tick were thoroughly drenched and his bed tick thrown into the sea, leaving him a hard bed for the remainder of the voyage.

Sensing the despondency around them, Thea took her book of fairy tales by Hans Christian Andersen and walked around the deck, stopping at every area where children were present and inviting them to come to a place near one of the stoves to listen to her read. One by one the children, along with many mothers, fell in behind her. When Thea was tired of reading one of the mothers or an older child would take her place. Some wished they had thought of this earlier in the voyage.

The passengers below deck were mostly Danish or Norwegian, but there was one very large family from Finland. It included seven children, ranging from a tiny infant to a girl of perhaps twelve, and their parents, as well as two older men believed to be uncles. When the older children joined in the reading group Thea knew that the Finnish children did not fully understand what was being read to them, but they didn't seem to mind.

And then came the day when land was sighted. Barely visible in the distance was the coast of Newfoundland and then Nova Scotia. In the dawn of the next day the ship slipped into New York Harbor, and by noon the passengers of the *Norge* out of Copenhagen, Denmark, stood on solid ground at the entrance to Ellis Island. It was April 12, 1893.

Mary and Thea struggled with the baggage while they dragged the American trunk, piled high with quilts and other bundles. John tried to help, but his efforts did little in the way of relieving the burden; he was so weak it was enough to put one foot in front of the other.

Mary Inga was put in charge of her brother and small sister, much to Peter's dismay, since he thought of himself as a grown-up now. He screwed up his face and lifted the basket he carried even higher.

A ship's steward came up behind them, relieving the women of the trunk and directing them into the correct line. There were hundreds of people, all from different places and speaking different languages, being shuffled about. Finding a spot near a wall, the steward slid the trunk against it. He directed the others to pile their loads on top and to leave the two oldest children to keep watch over their belongings and little Dora while John, Mary, and Thea waited in line with the inspection papers to be cleared and stamped. It wasn't until then that Mary realized the names written on the papers she held were not their own. Why were Per and Marie's names written on them?

"John, look here," she said. "Per and Marie...their names are written on our inspection papers."

"What? How can this be?" Then he remembered. "Their names were on the tickets, remember?"

"Yes," said Mary, "but we gave them our names and explained about your uncle telling Per to give the tickets to us when we were at the Immigrant Hotel in Copenhagen."

"That's true, but there must have been some confusion. We will have to be Per and Mary for now," John said weakly.

"But, John, we are not them." Mary was close to tears. "How can we pretend to be?"

"We will! We must!"

By the time their turn came it was unclear to themselves just who they were with any certainty, but in moments they were passed on to purchase their train tickets for Iowa and to exchange their Danish kronen for American dollars. When they learned the train was not due for two days and Mary noticed that others were preparing to wait there and to sleep on the floor, she suggested it to John. He was having none of it. Though his strength was nearly gone, he insisted they get away before Dora started to cough and her tuberculosis be discovered. When Mary spotted the young steward who'd helped them earlier she sent Thea to hurry after him and seek his help.

When Thea and the steward returned they brought with them a woman who worked there as a guide. She spoke both Danish and German and suggested they wait there until she could see about accommodations. She was most helpful, but John, still gripped in fear, wanted to go away from this place. The woman looked questioningly at Mary when John said, "Nein, we will go with you now."

"Very well," she said, "but it would be much better for you to wait for me here where you can rest."

"Nein," he repeated, and they followed her with all their belongings as the steward took the lead with the American trunk.

On the dock once more the woman hailed a wagon driver, speaking to him in English. Returning to them she said, "This man knows of a room you can have for two days. It is not far from the train depot. He has agreed to fetch you and your belongings and take you to catch the train." She paused, "Do you have money?"

"*Ja*. How much?"

"The room will be two American dollars for the two days, and the driver will charge you two American dollars to take you there and pick you up. I know it's a little steep but you didn't give me an opportunity to shop around for a better price."

"I know," said John. "We are much obliged."

"Did you exchange your kronen for American dollars?" she asked.

"*Ja*," John said. "I exchanged it when I purchased our train tickets for Iowa, and it was a fair exchange. The man selling the tickets was good enough to show me the exchange schedule."

"Good," the woman said, "because sometimes they cheat you at the exchanges on the Island."

Mary spoke up. "Could you tell us where we can buy milk and fruit?"

The woman said, "I will tell the driver what you need and he will stop at a market."

They had traveled a short while when the driver pulled to the curb in front of a market and got down. He held out a dollar bill, then put it back in his pocket and held his empty hand out to John, who knew what the driver wanted. He handed the driver a dollar. The man went inside the market and came out with two glass bottles of milk and some apples wrapped in red papers. The journey resumed, and a short time later the wagon stopped in front of a run-down, two-story house. Two children played on the porch that spread across its front.

The driver got down and went up the stairs to the door and knocked.

A tired-looking woman answered and the driver spoke to her while he pointed to his wagon. When he came back he motioned for them to get down while he began unloading their belongings and carried them up the steps and through the door. The woman started up a flight of stairs and motioned for them to follow. At the head of the stairs she opened a door to a room with three beds. They looked clean, although the covers appeared thin and worn. But it didn't matter. As soon as John paid the woman for the room, the door was closed and they all collapsed on a bed, too tired to think about to-morrow or to even rejoice about their arrival in this new land.

The two dollars included breakfast and supper, and at seven o'clock the next morning they heard a light tapping on their door. Mary opened it to find the woman, looking as tired as she had the evening before, standing there. "Breakfast will be ready in half an hour." But seeing that Mary did not understand she made a gesture of putting something in her mouth and Mary smiled, saying "*Ja*" the universal word for 'Yes, I see'."

Breakfast was simple. A bowl of hot porridge served with milk and sugar—and how good it tasted! It was the first food John had been able to enjoy in a long time. The woman smiled at seeing how much they enjoyed the simple fare.

The wagon arrived just after dawn the following day, and the driver loaded their belongings while the family made ready to go to the train. The woman had fixed the porridge early so they could eat before leaving and as they started toward the wagon she handed Mary a bundle and made a gesture of eating and Mary understood. The woman was sending them off with food to eat on the train. Smiling, she put her hand on the woman's shoulder in a gesture of thank-you as she said, *"Danke."*

Six days on the train and then they would be in Iowa.

The train car where they were to sit was crowded mostly with emigrants from other countries. There were two families they knew from the ship. Both were from Denmark. A German man and his wife who they recognized from the ship's first class section sat rigidly in the farthest seat forward.

Sitting in the straight-backed seats for hours on end while the train rocked and jerked did little for John, who was still in a weakened state, or for Mary, whose time for delivery grew nearer. What a blessing, she thought, that Thea was with them—what would they have done without her help!

Little Dora lay across John's knees with her small head in Mary's crowded lap. Mary stroked her hair tenderly and whispered to John, "She's gotten so pale again. It will be good to settle into a home where she can run and play. I wonder how long it will be before we get there."

"Tomorrow, in the afternoon. I asked the porter."

"John, how did you ask him? He doesn't understand us."

"No, but I asked the German fellow from first class and he asked the porter. He speaks English as well as German."

"You must be feeling better," said Mary.

"Some," he said, "but not much. I'll be glad to get off this confounded train."

The wind was blowing when the train lumbered to a stop before a low wooden station set back slightly from a long platform. The name of Emmetsburg was painted on its front.

John, Mary, and little Dora were the last to get off and Mary quickly pulled her shawl about Dora, shielding her from the wind, but not before she started to cough. Her cough had been getting steadily worse, catching the attention of the other passengers, but Mary had offered no explanation.

Leaving the trunk on the platform they hurried toward the station door only to be met by a man who stood scowling in the doorway and blocking their entrance. He had a slight build and eyes the color of steel, and just as cold. His voice trembled slightly as he spoke.

"You John Adamson?"

"*Ja*… I am John Adamson. You are my uncle then? It is good to meet you. I am sorry I have not been well… at sea, I…" He tried to explain, knowing how thin and gaunt he must appear.

"I can see that," said the man, "You'll not be any use to me,"

"But, Uncle…"

"Na…I can't use a bunch like you, relation or not." He pointed to Mary's obvious condition. "And there'll be another mouth to feed."

"Can you at least put us up for a time?" John asked. "I will be able to work soon."

"Got nowhere to put you!" The man shouldered his way between them, leaving them standing on the platform.

For a moment, no one spoke and then Peter said, "He is a bad man."

"Peter," said Mary, "you must not say that." But in her heart Mary knew it was true. She looked at John, who just stood there, dumbfounded, watching the uncle walk to the end of the platform where a mule and wagon waited. He saw him speak briefly to another man before driving away.

Mary shouted above the sound of the howling wind and the train as it left the station. "What should we do? We've come so far…"

Thea led them through the station door to a wooden bench. "We couldn't stand out there in the wind," she said. "We need to talk about what we are going to do. At least it's warm in here."

Just at that moment the station door opened and a short, stocky man with a pleasant smile came in and walked up to John. Holding out his hand he said, "How do? I am Andrew Peterson." He spoke in Norwegian and then switched to broken Danish.

John shook the man's hand, puzzled. "John Adamson."

"*Ja*, I know. I know your uncle. I work for him, and he is a hard man."

By this time, the numbness had worn away and John was angry. "He is more than hard, he is a weasel."

"I agree," said the man. "I know of a place where you can live until you get back on your feet. It isn't much, but it'd be a roof over your heads. Do you want to see it before you make up your mind?"

"Nein," said John. "Can you take us there? I can pay you."

"I won't take your money," said Andrew. "Wait here where it's warm while I haul you some hay for a bed and see about finding you some kind of a stove." And with that he hurried off.

John, knowing the Norwegian word for thank-you, called after him, "*Mange takk*."

Andrew Peterson, without turning, raised his hand in acknowledgement.

The station master came from behind his desk, where he had been busy on the teletype, to tell them in broken Danish that he was leaving for the day and that he wished they would lock the door behind them when Andrew came back for them. He had also set a pot of coffee on the potbellied stove that sat in the corner and indicated that they should turn the damper down before leaving. They thanked him for his kindness.

Before long the coffee began to boil. Mary pulled it away from the hottest spot on the stove to simmer to its full richness. She placed slices of sausage and cheese onto pieces of flat bro and handed one to everyone. Only little Dora refused to eat, burying her face in her mother's skirt. Her parents exchanged worried looks. The coffee tasted good, even to Mary Inga and Peter, who let it cool in their tin cups before drinking.

It was dusk before Andrew Peterson returned for them and helped load the wagon. The wind had died down, but the air was cold. Mary sat with Thea and the children in the bed of the wagon, a quilt pulled tight around them. The road was full of chuckholes from the winter's frost boils, and Andrew Peterson wove his way over the road so as to miss them.

Darkness had settled in by the time they reached the small, rough-board shack. Mary guessed it had once been a chicken coop. There was evidence of it having been shoveled out and swept, although cobwebs still hung from the pole rafters. A line of open-faced boxes was fastened to one wall that she suspected were old nests. A pile of clean straw was stacked at one end, and at the other a small bachelor stove was set with a stovepipe going through the wall. Near it stood a shuttle of coal and a pail of water.

By the time they were all inside and the wagon was unloaded there was little room to move about, but they were glad for the shelter and the provisions this kind man had afforded.

Andrew Peterson wished them well and said he would look in on them the next day. The family's thanks were so great that he blushed with pleasure.

That night, despite their exhaustion, John and Mary lay awake and wondered what they would do now.

The morning streamed bright and sunny through a small lone window by the door. Mary had the fire started in the stove and the coffee on to boil before anyone else awoke. She was preparing a mustard plaster for Dora's chest when John opened his eyes and asked, "What are you doing?"

"I'm making a mustard plaster for Dora," Mary said. "Her breathing is so shallow and raspy."

"I hope it helps," John said. "She doesn't sound good."

"How are you feeling?" Mary asked. "You are still so pale."

Ignoring her question, he said, "I have to find work, and soon. The money we started with is nearly gone."

"You are in no condition to work at anything. Be sensible…"

"I have to or we'll starve. What have we left to eat, some moldy sausage, a little flat bro, a little cheese?"

"*Ja*, I know," said Mary, "but…"

"I have to work!"

Later that morning Andrew Peterson came by to see how they were getting along, and he was invited to sit on a box and have a cup of watered-down coffee. Mary set out a lone pastry she'd been saving for such an occasion only to see it covered with little green spots.

Mold. She quickly whisked it out of sight, but not before their guest saw it.

Andrew was not only a kind man, but a humorous one as well, telling some of the most outlandish stories. He was a bachelor and had living quarters in the little nearby town of Ruthven. When everyone kept calling him Mister Andrew Peterson, he asked them to please call him only Andrew. He brought them a bottle of milk, a large cabbage, and a pail of potatoes. He said that he hadn't known what to do with them before they spoiled and had thought of them. He acknowledged John's embarrassed smile when he thanked him, but Andrew knew their plight, and the very next day he came leading a cow.

Andrew had approached the uncle with an outlandish scheme.

After stripping one of the cow's quarters dry, he had asked the uncle what he intended to do with the cow, telling him she was dry in one quarter. After testing the quarter himself, the uncle agreed that he needed to get rid of her and agreed to sell Andrew the cow at a very cheap price.

When they heard the story John felt almost vindicated and told Andrew he would pay him for the cow as soon as he was able. Mary, however, was a little taken back by the lie that had earned them the cow.

Thea found a job in a restaurant, and the family breathed a sigh of relief, for now they knew they could at least eat. The wages were not much, but Thea could bring home the table and kitchen scraps; some of which were eaten by the family, but most of it went to the cow, who seemed to thrive on it.

They had been in Iowa less than a week, and little Dora was growing steadily weaker until John and Mary feared the worst. It was then that Andrew brought a small Irish woman to their door.

"Me name is Rose," said the woman. "I coom ta help with the wee one." Although they hadn't a notion what she was saying she made herself understood in action. She was little, like a bird, with flashing black eyes.

Looking beyond the others to the bed of straw Rose saw little Dora and hurried to her while Andrew explained how Rose was often summoned to help with the sick, calling her an angel.

Rose helped care for little Dora as best she could, but her small body was racked with coughing, and two days later little Dora Amelia Tora died.

John, still too weak and dehydrated, was unable to help with the burial preparations and had to accept the small wooden coffin their friend Andrew made. He lamented over what he thought were false hopes that Dora would get well. He wished they had stayed in

Abenraa, where life was good. He, of course, could not look beyond their present circumstances.

Dora Amelia Tora was buried in a small grave not far from their shanty's door, and John and Mary thought they would never cease grieving, but in time they did, looking back only on the joy little Dora had given them and not the sorrow.

John finally found a job in a chicken cannery, where he scalded the chickens once they were killed and plucked their feathers. The stench was more than he could stand and he didn't last even an hour, but rather than return home, a failure, he went from one place to another. Finally, a man he met named Jebbe Skow drove him to the railroad yards near Emmetsburg where he was promised a job beginning the following week. John returned home excitedly to find Mary in labor. Mary Inga had gone for Rose, and Peter sat on the ground by the door, his knees spread and his head in his hands.

Ruffling his hair, his father asked, "What is this? What has happened?"

"Ma is real sick," said Peter. "She made me go outside and sent Mary Inga to get Rose."

"Is Rose inside with your Ma?"

"*Ja*, so is Mary Inga but they won't let me in."

"Well," John said, "I guess us men will have to wait out here. I've been told before that a man has no place around a birthing."

"You mean Ma is birthing right now?"

"Probably."

"But I don't want none. I just want little Dora that's all.

"Well, I'm afraid that isn't possible," said John. "Dora is in heaven."

"I don't see why God needed her yet," said Peter. "He could have waited till she got big."

"God has a plan for all of us and it's a good plan, even if it doesn't always seem so good at the time."

Just then they heard a baby cry and Peter said, "Oh no, it's a crier." John chuckled at that.

They named the baby Emil. He was born just one month after little Dora died. It was the sixteenth day of May 1893.

John made arrangements with Jebbe Skow, who also worked on the railroad, to give him a ride in his buggy until John could earn enough to rent a house nearer to the railroad.

One evening, when Jebbe drove up to the Adamson's shanty with John, Thea was hanging clothes on a line they had strung between two posts. She looked up and Jebbe tipped his hat. Thea was introduced and a whirlwind courtship began. Jebbe was a widower and had one son who lived with him. His name was Edward, and from the moment she and Jebbe were married it was understood that Edward would be catered to. Thea and Edward got on quite well, he needing a mother and she needing to love a child. Thea learned that Edward's sister, Inga, had been given away as an infant when their mother died. When Thea tried to coax Jebbe into getting the baby back for her to raise, he wouldn't hear of it.

Jebbe had a place in Ruthven with a few acres where he raised enough corn to feed some hogs and a cow. It was Thea's job to take care of it all.

As soon as John was able he moved his family to an old, dilapidated farmhouse and sharecropped the small acreage while he continued to work at the railroad. The family had gotten a bred sow, and when it was time for her to farrow she somehow got out of her pen and came up to the door of the house. Peter heard the commotion and opened the door. The pig grunted, turned around, and went down the stairs. Then she looked around as if to make sure he was following her, and discovering that he wasn't, went back up the stairs. Mary came to the door and suspected what the pig wanted. She followed her back to her pen where she began to have her piglets almost immediately. She had had all seven by the time John came home from work, and Peter and Mary Inga ran to tell him about it.

"Pa...we got baby pigs." Mary Inga cried. "Seven of them."

"Nay...we only got six," Peter corrected. "One died, but she came right up to the house and got us when she was ready to have them."

"What did I tell you about lying," said John. "Go in and get the strap."

"But, Pa," he said, "I'm not lying."

"Do as I said, Peter, and be quick about it," said John.

Mary Inga ran to the house to get their mother to prove to their father that Peter wasn't lying.

Wiping her hands on her apron, Mary came down the stairs into the yard and faced her husband. "Peter is telling the truth," she said. "The sow did come to the house to get us."

"Are you sure she has no more?" John asked. "Seven is a small litter."

"Six, Pa, one died," Peter blurted.

"*Ja*...six." He looked at Mary.

"I'm certain—there were only seven, John," she said.

He said no more and strode to the house, kicking a clod of dirt.

After spending the winter in the small shack that Andrew had provided it was good to be in a house although the wind entered the many cracks and crevices and seemed to blow constantly. Winter turned to summer with little spring in between, and by the time they were settled in the house it was hot but still windy. There'd been little rain and the earth was bone-dry.

Mary and the children dug up a patch of dry sod to ready a place for a garden. As Mary dug, the children shook the dry clumps of grass free of dirt and threw them into a pile to feed the pigs. Once the soil was dug loose she made rows with a stick and the children planted the seeds. The garden seeds she'd brought from their homeland took well in the American soil, but when the shallow well began to go dry the precious garden had to be watered by the cupful around each plant. They mounded the dirt around the plants, hoping to keep the water from escaping from where it was needed. Soapy dishwater was used on the turnips and rutabagas in an attempt to keep then from getting wormy.

By fall, they had begun to harvest the root vegetables, putting them down in barrels of sand to be stored in the dilapidated root cellar. Earlier, Rose had come upon them digging holes in the ground to store their vegetables in as they had in Denmark. She'd watched for a time and then asked what they were doing. When she found out, she showed Mary the root cellar in the yard and its purpose. Anxious to learn American ways, Mary agreed to try it. She soon learned that the idea of the root cellar had come to America from Europe. Tanta Dorthea had such a storage place in her house, but not as big as the ones in America. It was Thea who told her why they were so big.

"Jebbe told me it is where you go to hide when a tornado comes."

"A tornado," Mary asked. "What is a tornado?"

"It is a big wind that twists into a funnel and destroys houses and crops. If you see one coming," and Thea pointed off into the distance, "you must take the children and run to the root cellar and climb into it and fasten the door from the inside and stay there for a long time until you are sure it has passed."

Mary was horrified by the thought and told John of it when he returned from the railroad yard that evening.

"*Ja*, Andrew told me of it," he said, "but I didn't want to frighten you. I'm glad that Thea told you so you will know what to do."

"Know what to do?" said Mary. "You sound as though we can expect such a thing as this tornado. Why did we come to such a place? At home it was the Germans, and here tornadoes. At least the Germans did not twist through the air."

"Nein, nein, it is not like that," John said. "I am told it seldom happens and when it does you can see it coming. This is why I did not tell you…"

For weeks afterward Mary watched the sky, but when nothing happened she looked less and less, and soon she seldom thought about tornadoes.

The weather grew colder and the time to butcher drew near. John agonized over which hogs to keep and which to sell. He had already decided to give Andrew and Rose half a hog each, and he would keep one for meat and one for a farrowing hog. It was clear that the pig he'd bought was not thrifty, since she'd had such a small litter, and with one a runt besides. John decided to butcher the sow and the runt and then choose a good farrowing sow from among the rest and sell what was left.

Peter didn't want the sow to be butchered. She, after all, had come to get him when her babies were to be born. How could anyone butcher such a smart pig? But his protest was to no avail, and early the following week Jebbe and Thea came to help. Baby Christ, who had been born in October, was laid in the cradle. Mary Inga was put to attend to him while John and Jebbe got on with the butchering. Mary and Thea filled crocks with butchered pork, spreading salt between the layers and over the top to preserve it for future use. They fried some and used the melted fat for sealing the layers in another crock.

While the men ground the meat for sausage, the women scraped the inside of the intestines for sausage casings. Then they stuffed the casings full and tied off the ends, poking small holes in the length of each so they wouldn't burst in the boiling water as they cooked for hours.

Mary and John and the children went to Jebbe and Thea's to help when their hog was butchered just a week later. Peter and Mary Inga helped to scrape the sausage casings while Edward played with baby Christ and did nothing else but get in the way. John had spoken of it on their way home.

"Jebbe's boy is old enough to be of some help," he said, "but he's a lazy good-for-nothing."

"Thea says it's the way Jebbe has raised him," Mary said, "and he won't have it otherwise."

John rode with Jebbe or walked to and from the rail yard, and he was anxious to buy a team of horses. He could ride one to work and then use them for farm work. He traded one of the pigs and a bull calf, born that spring, for a team and a rickety wagon. The team wasn't much to look at. King was a gray with split hoofs and a tangled mane, while the other horse, a crooked-legged bay, was called Jim.

Winter hit with a vengeance, and more than once the family wondered about the wisdom of coming to this land, and then they thought of little Dora and what was happening all over Europe. They'd heard reports from those who had recently come from the homeland about one small country after another being swallowed up by the Germans and the unrest between Britain and Germany and Russia. Many felt that one day a world war would ensue.

They had never experienced a winter such as this, with the wind and the cold, and any fragment of wood not burned in the stove was shoved into a crack in the walls, as were scraps of cloth.

Andrew was a frequent, welcome visitor, and on occasion when he'd had too much to drink he was put to bed on a straw tick in a corner.

Mary's family in the old country was much on her mind, and she longed to hear more from them. Tanta Dorthea had written twice to say that everyone was well and to say that she had not succeeded in her quest to return Thea's child to her. Indeed, she had not even been given permission to see the child. Mary wished that Tanta Dorthea would write such news directly to Thea herself instead of asking her to do so, but to do it in an encouraging manner.

Anna wrote on occasion, always telling of what her Sophus had said about this or that and how disappointed he was that she was still not with child. Then one day a letter arrived with the news that she was expecting a child, and as much as Mary reprimanded herself for thinking such a thing, she wished dear Sophus had stayed disappointed.

Then a letter came from Lana, one that Mary had lived in dread of:

Our brothers are in fear of induction. Frederick and Heinrick both talk of America. I am afraid for them, as well as for Christian. I am not certain if it is even wise for me to write to you of it. These are frightening times, and I hate to speak ill of Anna's husband but I am uncomfortable even in his presence. Please pray for us, but especially for our brothers as we pray for you.

Your sister, Lana

Mary agonized over her family even more and prayed for her brothers as well as for her homeland.

An encouraging letter from the Captain quickened their hearts, even though they knew deep down that he was trying to cover the truth with soft words.

From Dora they'd heard nothing. For months she had not written.

It was nearly three years since they'd arrived in America, and Mary was due for the birth of her second child born in the new land.

The wind had been relentless for days, and Mary thought of the wind that had been raging when Dora Amelia Tora was born, when Anna had had to run to the Captain's for Dora and they had feared that John was lost in the storm. But those storms were seldom and nothing compared with these in Iowa. The wind blew the snow into drifts around the house, for which they were grateful since they helped to keep out the cold.

It was during such a storm that Mary went into labor with her fifth child. It was in the morning that she felt the first pains, and knowing what it meant, she added coal to the fire in the old iron cook stove and put on a kettle of stew.

Mary Inga was on the high stool near the stove working a cross-stitch pattern she'd just learned, while Peter and Emil crawled after one another, barking like dogs, until they nearly upset the stool.

Mary scolded them. "You boys settle down and play something quiet."

A sharp pain caused her to gasp

Mary Inga said to her mother. "Ma, are you alright?"

"*Ja*," said Mary. "You'll have a new brother or sister by the time the day is out."

"Should I go for Rose?"

"Nein. There should be no need."

But a few hours later Mary knew there was something wrong as she lay across a thick straw tick.

"Peter" she said, "dress warmly and get Rose. Hurry… before it gets dark. Be careful."

Peter's face turned pale. He knew there must be a great need for his mother to send him out in such a storm.

"But, Ma, shouldn't I go?" Mary Inga asked

"Nein," said Mary. "I might need you." She looked at Peter. "Be careful of the debris flying about."

When Rose and Peter returned, clinging together against the wind, they found Mary in great distress.

"I'm glad you've come," she said, "I can't…"

Rose said, "The wee babe be needin' turnin'. Dun you worry, lass. I've seen the likes of it many a time."

It was dark when John came home, and he knew what was happening by the children's faces and Mary's muffled cries from the room off the end of the kitchen. He asked Mary Inga, "Why is the door left open?"

"Rose wants the room to be warm for Ma when the baby comes."

"Rose is here then," he said. "Did you go after her?"

Peter spoke up. "I did, Pa, and it was windy."

"Still is. You might as well go to the barn with me, Pete. Chores need to be done." He took the lantern from the hook by the door and lit it. "Bring the pail, Pete." But as they started out, they heard a cry and John looked toward the room, concern on his face. Hesitating, he looked at Mary Inga. "Watch Emil so he doesn't go to his mother."

"I will, Pa," she said.

Nothing had changed when they returned to the house with the milk, so they ate supper. John sent the children to bed and sat at the table until he could stand it no longer. After feeding the fire, he put on his coat and went back to the barn.

He curried the horses until they shone despite their shaggy winter coats. He could still hear Mary's muffled cries when he went back to the house. He paced the floor worriedly until at last he heard a baby's cry. Shortly after, Rose came into the room. She lifted the kettle and poured the little that was in it into a basin. She glared at him and shook the empty kettle at him in reprimand before hurrying from the room. John quickly filled the kettle, put more coal on the fire, and pulled the kettle to the front. He knew it would take too long to heat. Why hadn't he thought to do it earlier when he knew both mother and baby needed to be washed? Moments later, Rose stuck her head through the doorway and motioned for him to come in.

Mary whispered, "Her name is Dora Amelia then?"

"*Ja*... Dora Amelia...that is a good name," said John.

It had snowed for days, but on the first clear day after Dora Amelia was born Jebbe's sleigh came in from the road and stopped before the porch, his team prancing and champing at the bit. It was clear they hadn't been used much through the long winter. Thea and baby Christ and Edward got out and climbed the steps to the porch while Jebbe turned the team towards the barn where he knew John would most likely be.

Mary heard them and threw open the door.

"Oh, Thea, I'm so glad you've come," she said as she reached for little Christ, who had grown since she'd seen him way back in November. Mary led the way to the cradle where Dora slept, and Thea gazed down at her exclaiming how beautiful she was. "Her name is appropriate," she said. "She looks so much like little Dora." She looked up at Mary. "I'm sorry," she said, "I shouldn't have said that."

"That's alright, Thea," said Mary. "She does look like her. I'm glad in a way...not that she takes her place, because she is who she is no matter what her name, but it sort of gives honor to both of them. I don't expect you to understand and I'm not sure that I do myself, but..."

Thea interrupted. "Oh, Mary, I do understand. You see...I see my little Dorthea there in your Dora Amelia's face as well." A tear slipped from her eye. "I wonder how she is...I miss her so much." When

Mary reached out a hand to touch Thea's shoulder her sister quickly brushed the tear away and changed the subject, as she always did if her daughter in Denmark was ever mentioned. Only once had she spoke of going to Denmark, wondering aloud if Tanta Dorthea would send her the fare, but Jebbe forbade it and it was never mentioned again.

Mary and Thea talked and shared news from home when Mary suddenly gave a start. "Oh my," she said, "the men will be in for supper and I haven't even started it."

Before long the women had boiled potatoes and made milk gravy. They pushed the pots to the back of the stove to keep warm while the pork was frying and carrots simmered in sugar syrup. They heard the men stomping the snow from their boots as they finished setting the table.

A couple of weeks later John came home with the news that Per and Marie and their family were coming to America. Uncle had sent Andrew to the rail yards to tell John.

"He's bringing them to stay with us for a week before he puts them to work," John said.

Mary was excited. "That's wonderful news. When will they come?"

"Andrew didn't say. I'll have to ask him."

"You don't look too excited about it. What's wrong?"

"Oh, I'm glad they are coming," John said, "but I was just thinking how fortunate Per has been. If the uncle doesn't like the looks of them they'll have a place to stay...with us. They won't have to live in a chicken coop."

"John, are you still holding a grudge against your brother because of your upbringing?" Mary asked. "It wasn't his doing."

"I know," he said.

The next day was Sunday, and Andrew came by with more news about Per and his family. He and John sat at the table having coffee while Mary set bread and cheese before them.

"I forgot to tell you when your brother is coming. Your uncle said it would be the second day of April. He will meet them and bring them here."

John laughed. "*Ja*, he will meet them to look them over. I wonder if they will pass the inspection?"

"John!" Mary admonished.

Andrew smiled. "Well, you know firsthand. I wonder if there are any more cows with a bad quarter in the herd?"

Mary couldn't help it when she joined John and Andrew in their laughter. Andrew slapped his leg as he roared and nearly fell off the chair. He was still chuckling when he put on his coat and cap to leave.

⸭————•·•————⸬

The damper had been left closed, and the house was full of smoke, so the doors and windows were wide open as Mary waved a tablecloth to clear the air when the uncle's open wagon arrived carrying Per and his family.

The uncle sat looking straight ahead while Marie and the children climbed from the wagon. Per handed down a large valise and jumped to the ground. Mary noticed the rest of their belongings, including their American trunk, were left in the wagon. She thought they must have passed the uncle's inspection and had to admit that they seemed to be in a far better condition than when they had arrived.

Peter and Mary Inga bounded down the stairs to start the hugging. Mary was right behind them with little Emil draped over one arm. She sought out Marie for her first embrace. As they greeted one another the uncle pulled away without a word. What a strange man, Mary thought.

Per looked toward the barn and asked, "Where is John?"

Peter said, "Pa is at the rail yard. He won't be home for a while."

Then Mary added, "No, but he will be so glad to see you, Per. He's been practically holding his breath until you got here. Come in, come in."

Peter and Louie disappeared to the barn, and Mary Inga and Anna found a corner where they talked and giggled.

After dinner, Per left the table to wander about until John came home. Mary and Marie washed the dishes. Knowing how tired Marie was, Mary suggested that she lie down to rest. Marie needed no further coaxing. Mary remembered the feeling after that long voyage aboard the ship.

The days seemed to fly by as Per and Marie filled them in on what was happening at home and passed Mary a stack of letters from her family. Mary slid them into an apron pocket to read later.

"We met with your family at Tanta Dorthea's," Marie said. "Everyone came but Anna's husband, and no one seemed too disappointed. They had a wonderful smorgasbord in our honor. Even the Captain was there. We asked about Dora since she'd been so kind to us but he was a bit evasive. He only said that she'd had to leave but that Bjorn was still with him. What do you suppose he meant?"

"I wonder…," Mary said.

John and Per spent long evenings planning for the future, sometimes including one another and sometimes not, but they each looked forward to a time of independence, of owning their own home and working their own land.

Before they knew it the week was up, and Andrew came with the uncle's wagon to pick them up. He was in a hurry, saying the uncle was in a foul way and anxious to get them started at their work.

Per and Marie gathered the children together and quickly got into the wagon. They said hurried good-byes and waved until they were out of sight.

That night, after the children were in bed, Mary sat with her knitting needles clicking while John stood looking through the window at the night sky. He turned and said, "*Ja*, I'm glad not to be working for the uncle. I think my brother and the rest of them will have 'a hard row to hoe' and I don't envy them."

"Yes, I'm afraid so," said Mary.

After John went to bed Mary took the letters from her pocket and began to read. She would give them to John when she was through. As she read, she found herself going from laughter over some silly thing someone had said or done to tears over a heart-rending situation.

She saved the letter from Frederick until last, somehow knowing the sadness it would hold and almost afraid to know what it said:

My dear sisters and all,

I hope this finds you well, as we are well. Elsie is still working at the hospital since we have no children. She sends her regards.

These are not happy times. I have recently received a notice to report for duty in the German army. All I could think of was to go to the Captain. He immediately put me in his employ, letting me keep our father's coal route but under his name and title. He wrote a letter to the German consulate stating that he wished to keep me in his hire because he had no one else and I was reliable.

I was grateful, but he said it was only a matter of time before his word would mean nothing. So far he has kept Bjorn from the army, but he, too, is in jeopardy. The Captain seems to recognize something different and menacing in what he calls the new Germany.

I cannot see any difference myself—they have always been dogs. I hate it that I must write this letter in German since I have been forced to forget how to write my own language—did I ever know how to write or read Danish? I was so young when our part of Denmark was occupied. I can remember but a few written words and a few spoken words except for words of endearment.

Lena tells me that she wrote to you about Heinrick's and my fear of being forced into the German army, and we wonder if her letter was intercepted. She mentioned that we were thinking of going to America. Right now they are keeping all younger men from leaving the country, and especially to America. Soon after that, I received my notice.

I have been trying to think of a way for you to let me know whether or not you got Lena's letter. It occurred to me that if you wrote to Tanta Dorthea and said that you either have or have not heard from Lena recently, by that I will know. I see her frequently.

I know that I am going on and on, but I feel it may be a long while before I can write again, unless of course someone else in the family goes to America. Elsie and I would like to go, but that possibility is not likely. I have many of our old friends on my coal route and they often ask about you.

Your brother, Frederick

A couple of months later John burst through the door with news of Per and his family.

"They have left the uncle, and with money from home, probably from Marie's family, have bought a small house and some land," he said. "I only hope they can see their way clear until spring when they can plant a crop. They have a few head of cattle, but not enough hay or feed to see them through."

"What will they do?" asked Mary.

"I don't know," John said. "I hope they saved enough money to feed themselves and the cattle."

"Have you talked to Per?"

"No, Andrew told me. The place they bought is way on the other side of Emmetsburg. I thought we would take a trip over there on Sunday."

"*Ja*," said Mary. "That would be nice."

When Sunday arrived they climbed into the wagon and started off. Mary brought a quilt for Per and Marie and knitted slippers for the children. Mary Inga had baked a cream cake the day before, and it sat in the back of the wagon bouncing up and down as they drove over the rough road.

Mary held baby Dora on the seat beside John. Looking back, she said, "Mary Inga, you had better hold that cake or there will be nothing left of it. Emil, you come and sit by your father and me." Emil did as he was told, nestling his head on her lap. He was soon asleep.

John was silent for a while and then said,"I wish we had our own place."

"We will one day," said Mary.

"I wonder when that day will be?"

"It's all in the Lord's timing. He knows when that will be and it will be just the right time."

John grinned. "And when do you think He'll let us know?"

"John…"

By the time they arrived everyone was eager to climb down from the wagon.

The house was two stories—two rooms down and two up. It was larger than the one they rented but every bit as drafty. Per and Marie and the children were anxious to show them around. When they were finished with dinner, Per crossed his arms on the table and looked at John. "You were fortunate that he turned you away," he said. "He's a hard man. There is no pleasing him. He may as well have held a whip."

"That's what I understood from Andrew," said John.

"The last straw was when he yelled at Marie, telling her what poor bread she made and to keep the children working harder. Marie wrote to her father, telling him of this hard man and then came a letter with enough money to buy this farm and to keep us until fall when the crop comes in."

"What did the uncle say when you left him?"

"A few harsh words about how ungrateful we were," Per said. "I intend to pay him the fare he sent us. And there is one thing I am grateful for...he told me that our sister no longer lives with our father and that she has a son though she has not married. Her son's name is Lauritz."

"Where does she live?" John asked.

"He said he didn't know, but I wonder." Per hesitated before saying, "We'll probably never know."

"Nei," said John, "but I have thought about our father. What a cruel man he was to turn us away; and then the uncle, his brother, cruel as well. I wonder what our grandfather was like."

"I don't know," said Per. "I have wondered the same."

It was getting late when they left, but they made it home before dark, bouncing up and down all the way. They were never so glad to be home.

Another winter passed, much as the winters before, and then spring came again, but to everyone's surprise it felt like spring this time. Warm, soft rains melted the last of the snow and around the old farmhouse a few spring flowers popped their heads through the soft earth. The garden and corn crop flourished, and then it was fall again. Unlike the beautiful spring, the summer had been hot and miserable, but at least the corncrib was overflowing, as was the root cellar.

Mary Inga, now twelve, and Peter, soon to be eleven, worked hard alongside their parents. Their father was not always an easy taskmaster, and Mary would sometimes have to step in. She could never quite understand how he could be so harsh with his children when he himself had suffered from such harshness as a child. However, along with his demands was praise—something he had never had until working for the Captain.

Emil was still too small to accomplish much, being only four years old, and was put to weeding in the garden and watching his sister Dora as she toddled about. Emil had taken to calling her Dory, and soon the name caught on with the whole family.

One day Andrew came by with some startling news

"Have you seen your brother lately?" he asked John.

"Not for a while," John said. "I was just thinking of making a trip out there now that I'm through in the field. I thought we'd go before it's time to butcher. Why do you ask?"

"Well, you better get over there and talk some sense into him," said Andrew.

"What he does is none of my business," said John.

"Wait until I tell you what he's planning."

John grinned. "Is he going to buy a cow with one quarter gone from the uncle?"

Andrew couldn't help but laugh, but then he turned serious again.

"John, I'm not joking around. Your brother is going to Mississippi."

"He's what?" said John. "Mississippi?"

"*Ja,* his crop didn't do well and this fellow came along and offered to buy his place. Gave Per some song and dance about how he had to move back to Iowa. He said it was because of some family problem, but how he'd had to leave Mississippi, where living was easy and the land was so terrible good." Andrew wiped his forehead with a faded bandana.

"I can't believe Per would do such a thing," said John.

"He told me himself," said Andrew, "and I thought you should know."

The next morning, Rose came to stay with the children while John and Mary mounted King and Jim and rode to Per's house.

They found Per by the shed. Mary left the men there and walked to the house. Marie met her at the door. "Mary," she said, "I'm so glad you've come."

Mary could see that she'd been crying. "Marie," she said, "what's this I hear about you selling the farm and going to Mississippi?"

She'd hardly gotten inside the house when Marie burst into tears. Her hands were over her face, which muffled her words. Mary led her to a chair and sat down in front of her and handed her a cloth to dry her eyes.

"Now, when you're ready," she said, "I want you to tell me what's going on here."

"Oh, Mary," Marie blubbered, "I don't want to go. I don't know what's gotten into Per. That man was a slick talker, and Per believes everything he said."

"Have you told him how you feel?" asked Mary.

"Yes…oh, yes, but he won't listen. He really thinks it is a grand opportunity."

"Has he already sold the farm?"

"Yes."

"And when are you supposed to go."

"Next week, by train. Per has already asked about a boxcar to take the stock and our belongings." Marie jumped up. "Oh dear. Where are my manners? The coffee is hot. Come to the table."

Just as Marie poured coffee and set on bread and cheese and a plate of pastries, the door opened and the men came in. Both were angry, and Per said in a stiff voice, "Sit down and have something to eat before you go."

"Before they go? They just got here," said Marie.

John tried to keep his voice soft as he spoke. "We have work to do at home."

After a hurried and silent lunch, John and Mary left, but not before Mary and Marie embraced. Mary spoke softly into her ear. "Think of it as a new adventure. I will be praying for you every day."

They rode in silence for a while, and John said, "That stubborn, pig-headed brother of mine. I can't believe he can be so stupid."

"John!"

"Well, can you think of anything so foolish?"

"No," said Mary. "But it is Marie and the children I feel so badly for. But, like I told Marie, look at it as a new adventure."

"*Ja*…a new adventure all right."

"Did you offer to help him load?"

"*Ja*," said John. "I said I would help him if he was determined to go, but he said no, that he could do it himself. So…let him do it himself."

John was angry about it for two more days. And then his thoughts turned to the task at hand: butchering. Jebbe and Thea came to help and, in turn, they went to help them. And then, before they knew it, snow began to fly.

Mary thought of Per and Marie and the children often and kept looking for a letter that never came. She prayed for them fervently always asking for a hedge of protection to surround them.

Two weeks after Dora's birthday, the seventh of February, Andrew came by with sobering news about Per and his family. He stomped the snow from his feet on the porch. Before he had a chance to knock, John opened the door.

"Andrew," he said, "we haven't seen you for a while. Come in. What brings you out on such a cold day?"

Leaving his coat on Andrew crossed to the warmth of the stove and rubbing his hands together he said. "I've got some news about your brother," he said.

John said impatiently, "What has he done now?"

Mary sat a cup of hot coffee on the table. "Sit down and drink this," she said. "What do you hear from Per and Marie? I keep expecting a letter, but…"

Andrew interrupted her. "You won't be getting a letter. They're back in Iowa."

John came to attention. "What? When did they come and where are they? I told him he was going on a wild goose chase."

"They are down and out, John," said Andrew. "They're living in the same old chicken coop where you folks had to stay when the uncle turned you away. I came to see if I could take this old bachelor stove out to them. I know you use it some, but they have no heat."

John turned white and Mary flushed before they reached for their coats and scarves. "I'll hitch the team," said John. "You'd better bring all the quilts we have." But Mary was one step ahead of him. She and Mary Inga were already stripping the beds of their covers when Andrew stopped John. "We can take my team and wagon," he said. "It's all ready to go. I'm afraid they'll freeze if we don't hurry."

Peter, a bit puzzled, asked, "Where are you going?"

Andrew supplied the answer. "To get your uncle."

As Andrew, John, and Mary hurried toward his wagon with the quilts. Mary Inga called after them, "I'll have dinner ready."

When they were safely back at John's house, Per kept saying how wrong he'd been, what a fool he was, until John stopped him. "It is true," he said, "you were foolish, but had it been me, I may have been just as foolish. I'm glad you're here and safe, but as soon as you are up to telling us about it, I am anxious to hear of your adventure."

That evening, Mary went to the barn to help with the chores. It was really an excuse to talk to John in private. Throwing her arms about his neck, she said, "I am proud of you, John Peter, you did a good thing to help your brother to feel better. He was feeling so much shame."

Pulling her arms loose and looking into her face, he grinned. "It is true what I said. I might have done as he did. Who's to know?"

The house was crowded with the two large families. At night, the floor was strewn with straw ticks and sleeping children. It was then that Per told them about their Mississippi experience.

"When we got there, a carriage was waiting to take us to a hotel, where we stayed for a few days until I bought two hundred and seven acres with a small house on it. I had to build a barn and a shed. Our only neighbors helped us with all we had to do, but they couldn't understand our language and we couldn't understand theirs, but we got on just fine. They were some of the nicest folks I've know. One day this fellow came riding up and told us not to associate with our neighbors. He called them names and said if we associated with them we'd be treated like them."

"Doesn't sound like a very nice man," said John. "How did your farming go?"

"Well, I soon discovered I'd bought a swamp, but even so we planted it to cotton. They said it could be done, but it's not like farming in Iowa or Denmark, I can tell you that. Then before we knew it, first one and then another of us came down with a kind of malaria. Marie and Sena almost died. If it hadn't been for our neighbors bringing Doctor Ray, who took the lot of us to his mineral springs resort where he nursed us back to health, I don't know what we would have done. All we had to pay him was my gold watch and our dog."

"Your dog?" asked John.

"*Ja*, he liked our dog. He was a good Christian man and he contacted the Woodman's Lodge in Ruthven for help and they sent us money for the train."

Mary squeezed Marie's hand. "Oh my," she said, "you certainly did have an adventure. But you must have been very sick—you are so thin."

"That was part of the treatment at the resort, near starvation," said Marie. "Once, Louie went to the kitchen for some food and Dr. Ray told him never to do it again or he would smack him with his slipper."

Per managed to get work at the railroad yard, and his plans were laid to save towards another place of their own. In the meantime, they stayed with John and his family.

That spring of 1898, John, Jebbe, and Mads Olson, a man they knew from the rail yard, and his son HC decided to go in search of homestead land in North Dakota.

John came home one evening and drew Mary aside. "Look at this," he said, pulling a paper from his pocket. It said that homestead land was being offered in North Dakota and that the railroad was offering free fare to anyone interested. The railroad had just finished building the Soo Line to the northern part of the state, not far from the Canadian border, and they wanted settlers

"It would be a good opportunity to have a place of our own," said John. "We could have one hundred and sixty acres if we proved up on it in three years."

"Prove up on it," said Mary. "What does that mean?"

"We would have to build a house of some kind and a shelter for whatever livestock we had and have so many acres planted. We'll have to find out more about it."

Mary looked into John's face and knew his mind was already set, that there would be no way to change his mind. And she wasn't sure she wanted to. It sounded like an opportunity that might never come again.

"But how will we do it?" she asked.

"Jebbe, HC, Mads, and I will go soon to find the land that we want and file a claim. Then we'll come back for our families."

"What about Per and Marie?"

"I've talked to Per, but he doesn't want to go. He said he's had enough adventure to last him a long time."

There was much to do. John and Per seeded the acres he farmed on shares with the land's owner. John would need his share of the feed and seed they'd harvest in the late summer to take to North Dakota, and some was needed for Per, who had decided to remain in the house in John's stead.

Mary and Marie and the children planted the garden. Mary wished she had planted more the last spring—food supplies were running low with so many mouths to feed—but they managed.

On one of the rare occasions when Mary was alone in the house, she went to the corner where their American trunk stood and lifted the lid. She picked up a small wooden box from where it was nestled among the delicately crocheted and embroidered fancy work she was saving for just the right time. She took a small journal from the box.

The Captain had given it to her before they left for America and told her to write about their lives there. It'd been some time since she'd done so, but now, sitting on the lid of the trunk, she wrote, bringing her journal up to date about themselves and the children and Per and Marie and all the new friends they'd made, and then she wrote about their new prospects for the future.

John is planning a trip to North Dakota to find homestead land. I know it is an opportunity to have land of our own, but wonder about the uncertainty it brings for tomorrow. It is May of 1898.

Soon after, Mary packed a valise and readied a supply of food for John. He had decided to take Jim, the crooked-legged bay, instead of King, since Jim was the younger and faster of the two, despite the crooked leg. Jebbe and Mads, he knew, would be taking better-looking horses, but no matter—Jim would keep up with them. They would likely have a lot of ground to cover to find the land that suited them.

In bed, the night before he was to leave, Mary reminded him, "Be sure there is water at hand until we can dig a well, and look to the soil...no rocks or clay."

"*Ja*, I know," said John, turning over.

"John, are you angry with me?" she asked. "I only meant to remind you."

Turning back towards her, John took her in his arms and said, "Nein...I worry about such a move. Is it the right thing to do? We are settled here...I have work and we are acquainted. There are other Danes here, people we understand."

"I know," said Mary, "but will the opportunity come again to own our own land?"

"To have our own land is what we've dreamed of," said John. Sleep was slow to come as he tossed and turned, still unsure of his decision. But the next day, John, Jebbe, Mads, and HC drew their pay from the rail yard and boarded the train. They would be back towards the latter part of June if all went well.

They had just walked their horses up the ramp and into the boxcar when they heard someone call, "Hey, boys, got room for one more?" It was Andrew Peterson.

"*Ja*, sure," John answered with a wide grin. "Decided to come along, did you?"

"I didn't even tell your uncle good-bye," said Andrew. "He crossed the line with me yesterday when he shorted me on my pay. Said I had to pay for a worn-out ax handle that broke." Andrew threw his bedroll and pack up the ramp. John grabbed it and stuffed it next to his own against the wall. Then Andrew led his black mare up and to one end of the car, tying her next to Jim. Bedrolls, saddles, and packs lay close together along the wall, with the horses tied at either end. Each man kept feed and a canvas water pail for his horse, while a barrel of water stood near the door. It was good to have Andrew along, good he'd decided to leave the uncle, John thought, as they settled in for the journey. None of them knew what to expect, except Jebbe, who always seemed to know everything whether he actually did or not.

There was plenty to do until John's return. The garden had already been planted, and they were certain that many of the vegetables would be ready to harvest before it was time to leave for North Dakota. It would be a whole year before they could expect any yield from the new land. Mary was feeling confident about their preparations when, without warning, the weather changed from warm spring days and soft gentle breezes to cold, blustery winds and hard rains. The ground turned to mud, and before it was over there was nothing left of the garden but some of the root crop.

When the sun finally returned Mary and Marie sank ankle-deep in the mud while trying to make rows for new seed. When they returned to the house, their feet were so caked with sticky mud that they could barely lift them as they walked and heard the oozing, sucking sound with every step.

There was also clothing to make ready, and Mary was grateful for Marie's help. As they worked, the two women talked of times in Denmark.

"Have you heard from any of the family lately?" Marie asked as she darned a sock.

"Not for some time, "said Mary. "I fear for them these days. It doesn't sound very good. More and more of the Danish way of life seems to be stripped from them, and it sounds as if Frederick and Heinrick will be forced into the German army. I especially worry about Frederick with his temper." Searching through the basket of mending for a matching sock, she asked Marie, "What do you hear from your family?"

"Mother writes about the dairy and what my sisters and brother are doing. They seldom write themselves. Father adds a little note at the end of Mother's letters sometimes. Mother said they are a bit nervous about the situation across the border. She asks about your family. She also says that she is praying for them. She said some of the churches over the boarder have been closed and one was destroyed. I asked her about the church where you and John were married, but she said she thought it was fine."

"I didn't know it had come to that," said Mary. "Why would they do such a terrible thing? They had already replaced most of our Danish clergy with their own who spoke only German."

"I'm sorry, Mary, I shouldn't have told you," said Marie.

"I'm glad you did," said Mary. "Now I know to pray as well." Taking up another sock she pushed the wooden knob inside to the toe and slid the needle through and through, crisscrossing the threads until the hole was mended and smooth. Then Mary held it quietly in her lap before saying, "I wish you were coming to North Dakota. I'm going to miss you. I missed you when you were in Mississippi. That must have been terrible for you."

"I'll miss you, too," said Marie. "But who knows? We may come later. You know Per—he does have itchy feet. And about Mississippi...it wasn't so bad until I got sick...and then the children.

I loved the people. They were so kind, and you should have heard them sing. They'd sway, keeping time to the songs they sang while they worked. Some were old spirituals, some they just made up as they went." Then Marie said, "My land, we need to start supper. I nearly lost myself in all our talking."

Mary hurriedly put the mending aside, saying, "My, yes, I'll start the fire. Wouldn't mind having supper on the porch, it'll be so hot in the house once supper is cooked."

The continuing heat had dried the mud until it cracked, and they were glad for every drop of rainwater they'd saved in barrels near the garden to water the new little shoots. Mary longed for the beets to grow tall enough so she could pluck a leaf here and there for a dish of boiled greens. She secretly wished and prayed for more than that. She worried that there would not be enough of the vegetable crop ready to harvest by the time they needed to leave for North Dakota. She knew they would have to be on their way before it became too cold. There would be much to do once they got there to prepare for winter. They had to build a house and shelter for the livestock, gather fuel…the list seemed endless.

Maybe it would be a nice fall, Mary thought. Maybe there would even be an Indian summer. But what if it wasn't? What if it was like the year before, when it snowed in September and stayed cold until May? That year, Mary Inga broke one of her father's shirts in half, it was so frozen, when she took it from the clothesline and bent it. What would they do if that happened again—freeze to death? Starve?

Mary Inga and Anne were busy, too, tying two new quilts. Peter and Louie each worked resoling their boots. They stretched one boot over another and then nailed new soles around the edges, trimming the edges with a sharp knife. Peter was getting good at resoling after once or twice feeling a misplaced nail come up and jab into his foot.

Per was in the barn sharpening sickles and plow shears—that is, when he wasn't tending the cattle. He was in a strange, pouty mood that he couldn't explain. All he knew was that he wanted to be left alone. When one of the boys showed up to help with something, he'd send them on their way. He'd told John that he did not want to go along to North Dakota, but his decision was eating at him. Had he been wrong?

One morning, Mary found her thoughts turning to Thea and how she was getting along with all that she had to do with Jebbe away. She was considering riding over to visit her when Thea arrived at the house in a cloud of dust, the back wheels of the wagon lifting as she turned into the yard. In one quick move she wound the reins about the brake lever and jumped to the ground and raced up the steps. Mary met her at the door, but before she could greet her sister Thea burst into tears and started to rant.

"I can't do it," she said. "The hogs… the cows…milking. I lost two baby calves in that awful mud. My garden is ruined, and I can't get anything ready to go to homestead." Without pausing for breath, she asked, "When will we butcher? How will we do that and get to Dakota before the snow flies? I'm not going…that's all there is to it. I'm not going." And she threw herself into Mary's arms.

"There, my girl," said Mary. "I'll go along with you to help. We'll have it done in no time at all, but first come in and have a cup of coffee."

"I can't be long, little Christ is with Edward."

"Mary Inga, you and Peter can come along to help." Mary asked Marie, "Do you mind watching Emil and Dora for the day?"

"Nei," she said. "Anne and Louie can go to help as well. Don't worry if you can't get back until tomorrow. You'd better each take a quilt, just in case."

Mary Inga and Anne worked on the mending, and Peter and Louie worked in the barn. Peter noticed Edward standing by the corral, his elbows leaning on the rail and his head bent as he chewed on a straw. Peter hollered, "Ed…what are you doing? Come help us!"

Edward looked toward Peter and growled, "I don't have to. Pa says I just have to see that things get done."

Peter looked at Louie and without a word they started for Edward. Edward took one look at their faces and knew their intent. He backed away and said, "Look here…you leave me alone…this is my pa's place."

"This is your pa's, is it?" said Peter. "Then why aren't you doing the chores while he's gone?"

Edward sneered. "That's Thea's job. It was her idea to go over and get your Ma to help. Why'd you come along anyhow?"

Louie grabbed Peter's arm as he drew back, ready to swing. "Pete," he said, "he ain't worth it."

"What'd you mean by that? Pa said…" but Edward said no more. One look at his cousins said it all.

Peter and Louie, with Edward between them, headed for the barn. Once inside, Louie handed Edward a shovel and the three of them shoveled manure from the gutters, pitching it to the manure pile outside the door.

In the house, everyone continued to work while catching up on the latest news. Marie mentioned the plight of their homeland and then wished she'd said nothing when Thea burst into tears.

"Did anyone say anything about my baby?" she asked. "Did they say anything about my Dorthea? It's been a long time since I've heard. When Tanta Dorthea writes, she just says the same thing over and over; that she's trying to do something about it and not to worry, but it's been a long time since she's written. I just try not to think about it, push it out of my mind like it never happened. But at times like this it all comes back. Jebb gets so impatient with me, but look what he's done with his own daughter—and he had a choice."

Mary rushed to her side and held her as she sobbed.

Trying to comfort her sister, she said, "Thea, I know how it hurts to lose a child. There is nothing to take away the pain, but...."

Drawing away, Thea whispered. "No! It's not the same. Little Dora died from no fault of your own. I let my baby be taken from me. I should have stolen her away. I..." Just then the door opened and the boys trooped in. Thea turned to hide her tear-streaked face while Mary asked, "And what can we do for you, or need I ask? Hungry?"

In unison Peter and Louie answered, "Yes'm." while Edward stood looking at Thea's back with a scowl on his face. Mary ushered them to the table, ignoring Edward's sour look until he said, "Thea!" in a harsh tone.

"Edward! That is no way to speak to your mother," Mary said.

"She's is not my mother," he replied.

"You will not speak to her like that," said Mary. "She is not your slave."

Thea turned and started to look at Edward apologetically until Mary shot her a look of reproach. Then she straightened her shoulders and said, "Ed, behave yourself. I thought you and I were friends and Mary is right—I am not your slave. Do you understand?" Turning her attention to the others, she said, "I believe we all need something to eat."

Thea began to lay the table with bread, cheese, and pastries while Mary set out a dish of new butter and a pitcher of buttermilk. But when everyone else went to the table Edward marched out, slamming the door behind him.

Mary looked at Thea and started for the door, but Thea caught her arm.

"No, Mary, it's something I have to do," she said.

"Of course," said Mary. She sat down with the others while Thea went from the house.

Everyone was through eating and the table cleared but for Thea and Edward's plates when they came back in. Thea's jaw was set and she said nothing to anyone as she sat down. Edward wore the same scowl although there was a softening about his mouth that indicated that something Thea had said had gotten through to the spoiled young man. Only time would tell.

The next day before noon Thea said that she and Edward could handle what was left to do and that she would take Mary and the children home. As everyone climbed up into the wagon, Mary and Thea looked back for the boys and saw Louie and Peter standing at the side of the house with Edward. The two women looked at one another and smiled before Mary called, "Boys, it's time to go." She knew they had been warning Edward, but as they left him they delivered a playful punch, and Edward's face broke into a half-smile.

At home, they found Rose in the house with Marie. She hadn't been well and had lost some weight from her already-frail little body.

"Rose, I am so glad to see you," said Mary. "I've been wondering about you." Mary embraced the small woman who'd come to mean so much to her since that first day when Rose had come to help with little Dora. "I've been to see you, but always you were away from your home." As Mary held her friend she saw that tears had welled up in her dark eyes.

"You don't look well, Rose," she said, "and are those tears I see?"

"Nay, a wee bit under the weather I am," said Rose. "But tell me…be it true that you are going away?"

"*Ja*," said Mary. "John has gone to look for homestead land in North Dakota. If he finds what he wants we'll be going. That's one of the reasons I've wanted to see you, to ask if you would go with us."

"Aye, lass," said Rose. "When will you go?

"John expects to be back towards the end of June, and we would want to leave by the first of September. We'll hope to butcher by then. It will be early for butchering, but if we tend the meat—get it fried and put down in crocks and larded—we can keep it cool in the root cellar. We'll can some, but there won't be room for many jars. Per and Marie can butcher their hog later. We hope to have potatoes and rutabaga and some carrots and beets. If our garden hadn't been drowned out, we'd have more, but we should be alright for the winter."

"I'll have a wee bit to add meself," Rose grinned. "I trenched me garden."

The men were relieved when the train finally lumbered to a stop and they could unload their gear. First they led the horses down the ramp and into a makeshift corral. It was clear the horses were glad to be back on solid ground. They trotted the perimeter of the corral, tossing their heads and snorting. Jim was the first to lower himself to the ground and roll in the dirt, sending up a cloud of dust.

A short, stocky man stood behind a counter writing in a ledger when Jebbe opened the door to the station master's office and the four of them walked in.

"Howdy, boys, what can I do for you?" said the man.

Jebbe did the talking since he spoke the most English and understood even more.

"We come to find land," he said.

The man reached across the counter to shake their hands and introduced himself as Oliver Knapp. Then he came from behind the counter and stepped through the doorway to point toward the street beyond the corral and immigrant shack

"There is a store, a bank, and a land office," he said, "and soon there will be a blacksmith and livery. There are only a few houses now, but Bowbells is growing."

He told the men to drop their gear in the immigrant shack, where they could bunk until morning. HC got a fire going in the stove to boil coffee and fix supper—their first hot meal since leaving Iowa—while the others went to the corral to tend to the horses and carry water to a water trough inside the gate.

John and Andrew carried their supper outside to a broken wagon bed that was missing a wheel and settled themselves to eat as they looked out over the country and watched the sun dip to the horizon. It was the most beautiful sunset either had ever seen.

"It's nice country. I wonder where we'll find the piece of land we'll want to homestead," John mused.

"I'd like to run into somebody who's already found his homestead. He might know more than we do," said Andrew.

John's face broke into a half-grin. "Are you suggesting that we are what some call greenhorns, Andrew?"

"Not exactly," said Andrew. "But you've got to admit…aside from Jebbe, we're all pretty green." And they laughed.

"Well, I guess we'll find out tomorrow," said John. He stood up and started walking toward the shack. "You coming? We'd better get some sleep."

It was still dark when they started off the next morning and it was midmorning before they spotted a building in the distance. As they approached, they could see a shed beside a corral and a sod hut. The hut looked deserted until a man, pulling up his suspenders, stepped from a privy and walked toward them.

"Godag," the man said in Norwegian. The language was much like their Danish, and it was easy enough for the others to understand most of it, although Mads and HC were the only Norwegians among them.

Mads answered, "Godag, we have come from Iowa to find land. My name is Mads Olson and this is my son, HC" Pointing to John, he said, "And this is John Adamson." Then he introduced Andrew and Jebbe.

The man called toward the sod hut, "Mama, coom." The door swung open and a small woman with a child on her hip stepped out and smiled shyly at them.

"I am Ole Hanson and my wife is Inga. Tie your horses and come in for coffee." "Coming in for coffee," as they well knew, meant sitting down to a meal of one sort or another. Having coffee never meant just coffee to a Scandinavian.

Missus Olson said, "*Ja*, coom," and stepped back inside.

The hut was small and smelled of earth and cooking mixed together, but it was neat despite the dirt floor. Inga ladled fat potato *klub*s filled with pork into each bowl, along with some of the broth they'd been cooked in, and set them before their guests and her husband.

The men discussed the homestead situation while they ate. John asked Ole Hanson, "How long have you been here?"

"Near four years," he said. "I was just given the deed to my one hundred and sixty acres. You got to prove it up in three years, and I just made it. It isn't as easy as you might think. Three years sounds like a long time, but when you've got to build some kind of a dwelling and a shelter for your livestock—and that's the easy part—then plow the sod of eighty acres and let it lay over until the next season and plow it again, and then disk and harrow before you can seed and then wait for a crop to harvest. It isn't any easy do'in."

Mads looked at Ole Hanson. "My boy and I can each have a hundred and sixty acres I was told."

"You can," he said, "but if it was me, unless you got a passel of boys big enough to work, I'd start out with the first hundred and sixty and take up the other once you got one proved up."

Before Mads could respond Jebbe said, "Well, I've got some good machinery. It won't take me long to work up eighty, or even a hundred and sixty acres."

Ole Hanson caught John's eye and smiled with him. Anybody knew a blowhard when they heard one. It wasn't that John disliked Jebbe, exactly, although he didn't care much for the way he treated Thea.

Andrew asked a question. "Are there any parcels left to homestead around here Mister Hanson?"

"Nei," he said. "But east of here there is plenty of land left."

"We'd better get going," Jebbe urged, "before it gets any later, or should we break up here and go our own ways?"

"We agreed to stick together, Jebbe, for now anyway," John reminded him. "But you're right, we'd better get going." He turned to the Hansons. "We want to thank you,
manga takk, for the good food."

The Hansons answered in unison, "*Velbacomin*, you are welcome, come again."

Days passed with John crossing one rocky expanse after another, always with Mary's words haunting him:
Be sure there is water at hand until we can dig a well and look to the soil...no rocks or clay.

By this time the party had broken up and John and Andrew were left to their own devices. The two encountered other homesteaders, but to John's disappointment the parcels he was interested in were already proved up or spoken for.

They were already into the first week of June and the weather was turning warmer. They saw land already under the plow and wished it were theirs. Andrew was getting restless. "I wish we'd find our land soon," he said. "I'd like to cut some sod before we go back."

"Sod?" John asked. "Are you planning to build a soddy?"

"Seems the best thing to do. Not many trees about. Don't you think so?"

John scowled. "Haven't you noticed the awful smell in those soddies we've been in? I think I'll bring what lumber I can and build a shack if we find the land to build it on."

"A soddy's for me," said Andrew. "I think it'll be a lot warmer come winter."

Finally, east of Bowbells, John and Andrew rode onto the land they had been looking for. Near-level but for a knoll that looked beyond to a slough full of water, there wasn't a sign of a building or land being worked in any direction.

"What do you think, Andrew?" asked John. "It looks good to me. You could take the hundred and sixty to the east. We would have the land near that stony creek to contend with, but we would have water until we dug wells."

Andrew thought for a moment. "Yes, this is it. Now to find and stake the boundaries."

John was driving a stake at the southwestern corner when he spotted Mads and HC riding his way. As they rode up, Mads hollered, "John...I see you are driving my stake. I took the claim just south of you, so we'll be sharing that stake."

"Did you both take a claim?" John asked, but he could hear HC's grumbling in the background.

Mads sighed. "Nei...we thought on it and decided that Ole Hanson was right. We'll put it in HC's name and hope the parcel to the south will still be there when we're ready for it. It's only the two of us to prove it up, and taking on another...well, I doubt we could do it."

Andrew was stretched out on the ground chewing on a blade of grass with his hat pulled down over his eyes when he said, "I think you're making a mistake. I'd take it now while you have the chance. Folks will be coming like a flock of geese since there's a town nearby, less than a day's ride from here."

HC looked at Mads. "Father, I think he's right. We can do it. I know we can."

Mads was quiet for a time, thinking it over, and then he said, "Well, let's go pound some more stakes." And they mounted their horses and trotted off.

Andrew called after them. "Besides, Jebbe will have plenty of time to help you with his powerful machinery." And they all laughed.

John left Andrew, who had come prepared with a flat shovel sharpened to a fine edge for his sod cutting, and rode toward his own claim. He looked back at his friend, a short, stocky man with powerful arms and saw that he had already stacked a pile of sod. John briefly wondered if he should be doing the same, but then he dismissed the idea and rode on,

When John reached the spot where he'd driven his first stake he dismounted, pulled up a clod of grass, and examined the dirt clinging to its roots. Silt and loam sifted through his fingers…it was good earth, and as he looked out over the land he'd chosen, a warm feeling filled him and he thought of Mary. It was their land, or it would be once they'd proven it up. John walked in different directions, trying to decide the perfect place for their home site; once again he thought of Andrew digging sod and once again he dismissed the idea.

They decided they would go back to Bowbells to file their claims and head back to Iowa, but Jebbe hadn't been seen for some time and they were in a quandary whether to leave without him, since he might have already gone there himself, or wait. They had no idea where he was, nor was there any way of knowing if Jebbe knew where they were. It was mere chance that Mads and HC had found them. They decided to wait until the next morning.

Mads, HC, and John were gathered at Andrew's the next day, admiring his stack of sod, when they saw a rider in the distance. It was Jebbe, and it turned out that he had taken up land that adjoined

John's to the west. It was uncanny how they all had taken up land that bordered one another.

When Jebbe saw the pile of sod Andrew had dug he said, "You're not going to have one of those sod houses, are you?"

"I am, and I'll be snug and warm when you're freezing," Andrew replied.

Jebbe huffed. "You won't catch me living like a mole."

Mads spoke up. "I'm leaning toward a soddy myself and so is HC What about you, John?"

"Well, I'm afraid I have to agree with Jebbe," he said. "I don't think my stomach could take the smell of a soddy day in and day out."

HC ended the conversation by saying, "It's time to get going. We have to file our claims so we can get back to Iowa."

Mad's face lit up as he looked at his son like he was seeing him for the first time. "HC is right, he said. We had better get a move on," and he slapped his son on the back as they went toward their horses.

When they entered the land office to file their claims, they found the small room crowded with men who were arguing with a tall, skinny man standing behind a table at the front of the room. He was waving his arms and trying to explain something to the angry group of men.

"Listen men," he said. "This isn't getting us anywhere. The rule is…one parcel of one hundred and sixty acres for every man over the age of eighteen, and those parcels cannot be combined into a single conglomerate. It doesn't work that way. Every man has to prove up for himself."

"Well, it isn't that way east of here, in Minnesota," said a man with a German accent.

"Well, it is in this neck of the woods," said the tall man. "Maybe you should go back to Minnesota. I've got others to tend to." He turned his attention to John, who was nearest the table, while the angry group filed out.

Once all of their claims were filed they went into the store to see the prices of the items sold there and to meet the proprietor. He was shorter than the land agent but just as skinny. He wore a smile that stretched from ear to ear and was anxious to make their acquaintance. Speaking in Norwegian, he asked, "Have you taken claims near here?"

"*Ja*. We will go to bring our families from Iowa. We'll be back in the early fall," Mads answered.

"Good," said the man. "I will have more supplies by then."

They all shook hands and then started for the immigrant shack, hoping the group of men they had encountered in the land office wouldn't be there when they arrived. The other men's horses were nowhere in sight, so they unsaddled their horses and turned them into the corral before entering the shack.

Supper was eaten in the shade of the old wagon bed, and afterward as they sat drinking their coffee John lit his pipe and passed his tobacco around. The conversation was full of dreams and plans of their return to their homesteads.

"We'll need to cut hay for the livestock as soon as we come back to see them through the winter," Jebbe reminded them. But John said, "A man by the name of Swenson came by while I was staking the southwest corner and said he'd cut my hay on shares. He also said he'd pile it near where I showed him our barn would be. I figured it would be one less thing to do once we get here in the fall."

HC said, "I wish we could have run into that fella, but I guess we'll have time to do some haying once we come back."

Mary was anxiously awaiting John's return, and yet when he did finally ride into the yard it caught her by surprise. She dropped the basket of clothes she was gathering from off the line and ran toward him as he dismounted.

"John! I thought you were never coming!" she said. "Did you find land? What is it like? When will we…" The rest of her words were lost as John kissed her. Then he looked at her with despair written on his face.

"You didn't find what you were looking for…" Mary said.

"I'll tell you all about it after I've had some coffee," said John.

By this time the rest of the family had gathered as he went up the stairs and entered the kitchen.

John said, "Pete, take Jim to the barn and give him a good feed. Check him close for any sore spots from the saddle. It was too dark in the boxcar to see very well."

"Yes, Father," said Peter and he was gone.

"How was it with Jim? Did his crooked leg slow him up?" Per asked.

"Nei! Not at all."

John sat down at the table while Mary set a cup of coffee before him and a plate of bread, still warm from the oven, and butter to melt over it and a jar of preserves.

His face was solemn, but when Mary looked close into his eyes and saw the twinkle she said, "John Adamson! It's not true. You did find land!" John's face broke into a grin as she punched him playfully on the arm.

"*Ja*," he said, "I found good land: one hundred and sixty acres of silt and loam." Mary opened her mouth to speak but he answered her unspoken question. "There is water. We'll have to haul it from a creek until we dig a well, but it's there. It's good land, and not far from a town named Bowbells."

"This is good, but now we must hurry to be ready." Mary's face was flushed with anticipation.

The following weeks were so crowded with preparations for the move to North Dakota that when each night came, snores arose from every bed, a sign of utter exhaustion. Only the little ones, Emil and Dora and little John, Marie and Per's youngest, slept peacefully.

While Per and Marie's eldest son, Mads Peter, went to stay with Jebbe and Thea to help with their preparations, the rest of the family helped with the tasks at hand. John and Per were able to thresh enough feed to hopefully get them both through until the next fall, if they were careful, and enough seed to plant next spring. They wished they didn't have to share a full half with the land's owner, but that was what was agreed upon. The other half was divided between the two brothers.

One evening Per sat quietly smoking his pipe. Then he looked at John and said, "I've been thinking. It isn't really fair that I take half of the feed and the seed. After all, you were the one who rented this place on shares, not me."

"But you will need both since you're staying on," said John. "Besides, I have sold all but one cow and a heifer. I'll be taking my team and a pair of small hogs, but that's all. Ni, brother, you are not to worry. I will have enough."

"Alright then," said Per, "but if you change your mind…" And the two men put their pipes back in their mouths until John added. "*Ja*, and I will have hay."

It was too warm to butcher, but time was running short. Mary wondered why it couldn't be like the year before, when fall came early with a heavy frost and then turned to an Indian summer, but it hadn't—it was still hot and it was already September. Mary was bemoaning the fact as she and Marie prepared supper one evening, and Marie, who had been quiet and thoughtful, said, "There is enough salt pork to last until you could butcher a hog in the winter and there will no doubt be game—rabbits, pheasants, and perhaps even deer."

Mary stopped peeling a potato and looked at Marie. "You're right," she said, "but what about you? If we take all the salt pork you'll have none for yourselves."

"We will butcher after you leave, so we'll have plenty," said Marie. "I hate to see you go, because I will miss you, but I know that since you are going you cannot wait too long."

With an unpeeled potato in one hand and a paring knife in the other Mary put her arms about Marie. "You are so dear, *manga tukk*."

"What a blessing," Mary told John that night. "We won't have to worry ourselves about butchering in this heat and I have enough potatoes and rutabagas and some other vegetables. We won't have all the fine things we are used to," she grinned, "but we'll manage. We will have sausage and cheese for the journey and bread and hard tack, of course. We'll manage!"

"*Ja*, and did I tell you," John said, "Agnes will come fresh in May so we will have milk for the table until well into March—that will help to feed us. Agnes is a good cow."

Mary was worried about Rose. They had tried to visit her, but she had not been home, so when Andrew came to see how their preparations were going for the move to North Dakota, she asked, "Andrew, have you seen Rose?"

"Nei! Not for a time," he said. "I will stop to see her on the way home, to see if she is ready to go."

The following day, Andrew rode into the yard, his face ashen.

"Andrew, what's wrong?" Mary asked. But she knew without being told.

"It's Rose," he said. "I went to see her. She was in her bed. She could barely speak, but she said, 'Tell Mary I cannot go.' I wanted to take her to Doc Hansen, but she refused. I hurried after him anyhow, but when we got back it was too late. She was gone."

"Oh nei, nei, nei... not Rose!" Mary buried her face in her hands and wept.

John had seen Andrew by the house and came from the barn to greet him, but as he came closer he saw that Mary was in tears. "What has happened?" he asked. "Why are you crying?" He looked at Andrew for the answer.

"It's Rose," said Andrew. "She's died. You knew she hadn't been feeling well?"

"*Ja!*" said John. "She was so thin, but I never thought...we will surely miss her."

Mary turned her tear-streaked face to John. "I was so looking forward to her going with us and she was so excited," she said. "I should have known she was sick. I should have helped her to get well. Perhaps..."

Andrew rested a hand on her shoulder. "Nei! There was nothing you could have done. Doc Hansen said he was surprised she lasted as long as she did but that she didn't want anyone to know."

Mary smiled through her tears. "*Ja!* It was not meant to be and I know she is singing with the angels in heaven."

That night, when everyone else was asleep, Mary crept to the trunk. She lifted the lid and put her hand to where the little journal lay and drew it out. Then, by a window where the moon shone through, she opened the journal and wrote:

Rose has died and I wish I could have told her how grateful we are for all she has done. What would we have done had she not come like an angel when we first came from the old country, when John and our little Dora were so sick?

Mary put the journal back in the trunk and went back to bed, but thoughts of Rose kept sleep from coming until it was nearly dawn.

The days following Rose's funeral were hectic, but at last they were ready. It was decided that Pete and Edward would ride in the boxcar with the men, while the women and other children would travel in the coach. It would take three long days and nights to reach the homestead.

It was hard to say good-bye to Per and Marie and the children. Per shouted from the platform as the iron wheels on the tracks began to turn, "Perhaps next summer, bro." John leaned from the doorway of the boxcar and waved as his brother and his family grew smaller in the distance.

North Dakota was not what Mary had expected, and yet she wasn't certain just what she had thought it would be. It wasn't as flat and barren as Iowa—although there had been a certain beauty there—but here the land seemed to lie in the familiar folds of Denmark

When they arrived in the station, it was too late in the day to start out for their homesteads. After everything was unloaded from the train and the horses were turned into the corral, they staked the cows in a nearby pasture to graze. The piglets, which had been just weaned from their mother only days before when the sow was sold, squealed as they were lifted from their crates and tethered with a thin rope tied around one hind leg. Almost immediately, they became hopelessly tangled.

Emil and Dora ran about, glad to be off the train and out of the stench of the railroad car. Hearing the piglets squeal, Emil poked his head from behind the immigrant shack and hollered, "There is a hog pen back here. Can we put the baby pigs in it?"

"By all means," said their mother. "That will be a good job for you and Dora, but watch that they don't get away from you. We haven't time to chase pigs."

Emil was sobered at the task of having such an important job, but Dora smiled as she ran after her brother, calling, "Wait for me."

By nightfall the men were settled where they would spend the night out-of-doors, and Mary and Thea and Mary Inga carried plates of food to them while Mads' wife filled their coffee cups. The women and children wrapped themselves in the quilts they had used to keep warm on the train and then lay down to sleep on a pile of musty straw inside the immigrant shack.

The sun was barely peaking above the horizon, sending a red glow heavenward into an otherwise dark sky, when they set off to build their dwelling. John had dismantled a corncrib and a hog pen in Iowa for the lumber, and Pete had worked for hours straightening the nails he'd pulled from the weathered wood to use again. John hoped that there was enough lumber to build a shack large enough to hold his family. He had brought a roll of tarpaper to cover the outside and ward off some of the cold, but he still worried that he'd made the wrong decision when he opposed the idea of a soddy. Now, it was too late, for the ground would be frozen before they could dig enough sod for the walls. Andrew had had the right idea—his sod was stacked and ready to use.

Emil and little Dora were left behind to watch over their possessions in the immigrant shack, and as they watched the others draw out of sight, Emil turned to Dora with a stern look on his face and said, "Now, Dory, we have to watch so no one takes any of our food or the piglets or anything else."

"Mil, who will take it?" she said.

Exasperated, he answered, "I don't know! We just gotta watch so nobody does."

There was no one else about. Emil and Dora turned their attention toward the buildings along the road some distance away. It was early, but a lantern's light shone through a window halfway up the street and they could hear the whinny of horses and the occasional bark of a dog. Dora moved closer to Emil, and he put his arm about her shoulders.

By the time the wagon reached the homestead, the sky had changed from blazing reds to soft pinks and violet to finally a bright, clear blue with the chill of fall.

John reined in the horses and turned to Mary. "What do you think of our land?" he asked.

She hesitated, looking first one way and then another, then her lower lip quivered and she whispered, "Oh, John, is it really ours?"

"It is," he said. "But first we must do what they call proving it up."

"What does that mean?"

"It means that we must build a dwelling to live in and one for our animals and then till and plant eighty acres in three years time."

"We can do it!" said Mary. "We will work hard and…" Her words were cut short when John's face suddenly paled. He turned his head in first one direction and then another.

"The hay…there is no hay," he said.

Mary stood up and looked about. "Where did you tell the man to stack it?"

"Do you see that stake?" he said. "I told him to stack the hay right there by where the barn will be." His face was now crimson with anger as he jumped from the wagon and hurried toward the spot. He was glad everyone else had gone to their own parcels. He didn't feel like facing them just now after all his bragging about what a good arrangement he had made with that stranger to cut his hay on shares. On shares indeed! The scoundrel had taken it all—just a few wisps were scattered about. He turned to Pete and vented his anger.

"Get that lumber unloaded and start scraping what hay there is together," he said. "Don't just stand there, get busy."

Mary and Mary Inga jumped from the wagon and began hurrying about, gathering as much of the scattered hay as possible. Then Mary took the scythe from the wagon and went off in a direction where she saw a stand of tall grass—any little bit would help.

John and Pete had the perimeter of the shack laid out and the uprights in place by noon, working at a feverish pace as John vented his lingering anger.

There was little time taken for a noon meal of bread, cheese, and cold coffee before the rest of the framing began. Then the stringers were laid in place for the roof, using a glass jar half-full of water to determine the levelness of the pitch. The walls of the shack were begun just as the sun hovered over the horizon. Before they knew it, it was time to start back to Bowbells.

Mary nodded toward a small stack of hay they had gathered and said, "As soon as the grass I have cut is dry, there will be more." John remained silent.

At the immigrant shack everyone but Andrew was there, and Mads' wife and Thea had started supper. Mary breathed a sigh of relief and rubbed the small of her back.

She had awakened that morning feeling queasy. By the afternoon, she felt that she might faint at any moment. She knew she was with child again, but had not told John yet. She wanted to wait until they were settled. After all, it would be June before the new little member would join their family. Mary felt relieved that at least one of them would be snug and warm throughout the coming winter. The whole day she had thought of little else. She worried that they wouldn't have enough hay for the livestock or enough fuel for their fire. The walls of the shack were too thin to keep out much of the cold. Why hadn't they waited until spring? But it was too late to think of such things now...they were here and somehow they had to survive.

Early the following afternoon saw the shack ready enough for the family to move their belongings from the immigrant shack and begin their life of homesteading. The Skows were not so fortunate since Edward had not proven to be as capable as Jebbe would have liked. Thea helped where she could, but admonished Jebbe rather than Edward, saying. "If you'd raised him to be more responsible and showed him how to work instead of filling his head with all the nonsense you have..."

Jebbe merely grumbled in response. The following day he enlisted the help of the storekeeper's son in Bowbells and then moved Thea and Edward and the little ones to the homestead. He had purchased new lumber, which had been stacked where the shack was to sit even before they had arrived.

Mary woke early the next day and noticed that John was not beside her in their bed. As she sat up and looked about, she saw the children still sound asleep, snuggled deep in their covers with just their noses sticking out. She shivered from the cold and, drawing a quilt around her, she stepped into a pair of sheepskin slippers sitting on the dirt floor by the bed. The straw in the bed tick rattled as she stood up.

A small pile of wood sat by the potbellied stove, and Mary supposed John must have found it lying about somewhere. She hesitated to start a fire. What if there was no more wood to be found? Then she remembered that John had said there were some scrub trees along the bank of the creek. She decided to go later and bring back as much as she could find lying about. Pete could go and cut down the trees and she would help him saw them in lengths.

Once a fire was going, Mary set the coffeepot on to boil and grabbed her shawl from a peg by the door. She pulled it tightly about her and stepped outside. The air was crisp as she stood, looking out over the land, and then her gaze took in the figure of her husband. He was standing motionless with his hands at his sides, looking as she had out over the land, and she whispered, "Heavenly Father, help us to do these things that seem so insurmountable right now. I thank you for this land and for your grace."

As she watched her husband, Mary wondered about the uncertainty she felt about tomorrow.